LITERACY INSTRUCTION MATTERS

Practical evidence-based
classroom strategies to inspire
student readers and writers

Karen Filewych

Pembroke Publishers Limited

For you, teachers. Your work changes lives.

All books are a team effort.
A special thanks to:
- The readers of my early drafts— Cheryl, Katrina, Dan, and Mom—whose timely feedback added both depth and insight.
- The Pembroke team: Mary Macchiusi, my publisher, for your ongoing support; Jennifer Dinsmore, my editor; and the rest of the Pembroke staff, whose attention to detail and behind-the-scenes efforts are very much appreciated.

© **2025 Pembroke Publishers**
538 Hood Road
Markham, Ontario, Canada L3R 3K9
www.pembrokepublishers.com

Funded by the Government of Canada
Financé par le gouvernement du Canada | Canadä

ONTARIO CREATES

Library and Archives Canada Cataloguing in Publication

Title: Literacy instruction matters : practical evidence-based classroom strategies to inspire student readers and writers / Karen Filewych.

Names: Filewych, Karen, author

Description: Includes bibliographical references and index.

Identifiers: Canadiana (print) 20250102978 | Canadiana (ebook) 20250102986 | ISBN 9781551383712 (softcover) | ISBN 9781551389714 (PDF)

Subjects: LCSH: Language arts.

Classification: LCC LB1576 .F55 2025 | DDC 372.6/044—dc23

Editor: Jennifer Dinsmore, Alison Parker
Cover Design: John Zehethofer
Typesetting: Jay Tee Graphics Ltd.

Printed and bound in Canada
9 8 7 6 5 4 3 2 1

Contents

Introduction: "Where Do I Begin?"

"One child, one teacher, one pen and one book can change the world."
— Malala Yousafzai

Consider the marvel that is reading: the recognition that sounds are represented by letters... that letters combine to form words... that words are strung together to create meaningful sentences. The act of reading is likely an effortless process for you now. In fact, most of us take this complex skill for granted. And yet, you are reading the words on this page—at least in part—thanks to the literacy instruction of those teachers who taught you many years ago!

Imagine all that is going on inside the brain of a skilled reader: knowledge of the nature of print, decoding the words on the page, reading with fluency, an understanding of vocabulary, synthesizing information, making connections to the text, inferring the author's intent, and more! We take this skill of reading for granted *until* we become teachers ourselves and are asked to teach our students to read. And what about teaching writing? Although the skills of reading and writing are entwined, the teaching of writing has its own complexities and nuances.

What daunting tasks set before elementary teachers. And yet simultaneously, what a wonderful opportunity—giving students the gift of literacy. As teachers, we know we can impact students in many ways: their self-confidence, their views of learning, their understanding of themselves as learners, even their views of the world. But arguably the most impactful influence is literacy. Literacy skills enable students to function in the world. To communicate with others. To think. To learn. Our students will use their literacy skills every day of their lives.

Unfortunately, too many teachers graduate from university with few courses in literacy instruction. Surprisingly, some without any at all. We walk into post-secondary classrooms as students and leave as teachers. The day we are hired by a school is an exciting one to be sure. But along with that excitement comes many questions: *What grade level? How many students? Where is my classroom? What subjects will I teach?* If you are like most elementary teachers, your assignment includes language arts instruction. Naturally, we look to the language arts curriculum for guidance. Although this approach is often helpful and reassuring in other subject areas, the language arts curriculum is sometimes not as straightforward as many teachers hope. After all, the teaching of language and literacy is not a linear process. The six strands of language—*listening and speaking, reading and writing, viewing and representing*—are inextricably intertwined. We can't teach

Language arts curricula are titled differently depending on where you live. In Ontario, for example, the latest release is the *Language* curriculum. In Alberta, it is called *English Language Arts and Literature*. It most provinces, it is entitled *English Language Arts*. For ease throughout this resource, I will refer to it as the language arts curriculum.

one strand without the other, and we continually revisit the strands throughout the year—and from year to year. Planning for and teaching the outcomes of this spiral curriculum can therefore be quite challenging. There is not a checklist to follow and we certainly cannot divide the curriculum into units, as is the case in other subject areas.

In order for this book to be a meaningful and practical read, the chapters were arranged according to the various elements of language learning. As you use this resource, remember to consider the focus of each chapter as one element connected to all the others. In our classrooms, these elements should not be separated: they must work together to create the most effective literacy instruction and learning.

As an English Language Arts consultant, the most common question I received: *Where do I begin?* Although the language arts curriculum varies depending on where we live, strong pedagogy and practices for teaching language and literacy apply to all. Whether you are new to the elementary classroom, new to teaching language arts, or simply looking to improve your literacy instruction, this book endeavors to provide you with the foundations for building an effective, literacy-driven classroom, with practical suggestions grounded in research and strong pedagogy.

Now, an important caveat before we begin…

Although this book focuses on literacy instruction, I encourage you to keep your students at the forefront of your mind. As Brad Johnson and Hal Bowman (2021) emphasize in their book *Dear Teacher*,

> … while you do have high expectations for your students and want them to give their best, remember that they are human first, and when you focus on things like building relationships and patience, they will actually work harder and be more successful. Students work harder for teachers they like and who like them. (3)

As we will discuss throughout this book, there is much emotion tied to literacy learning. The more we consider our students as humans with lives beyond the classroom, the better we understand them and the better we can support them. In his book *Hidden Potential*, Adam Grant (2023) suggests, "It's about fostering a culture that allows all students to grow intellectually and thrive emotionally" (176). This sentence sets the tone for where we're headed with our literacy classrooms: *creating a culture where all students can grow intellectually and thrive emotionally*. I can't think of a worthier objective.

Think back to the teachers who have influenced you, those you remember fondly. Most likely, you remember them because of the relationships they built with you. I would venture to guess that these teachers took an interest in you as a person: they asked about you, they remembered things about you, perhaps they conversed with you about your interests. Relationships are key. So, as *you* strive to foster a culture where literacy learning flourishes, consider that what you see in your students is like an iceberg: only the tip. There is much more below the surface. To fully support students in their literacy learning, we must be cognizant of what might be below the surface affecting their attention, their perspectives and perceptions, and ultimately, their learning. They are, after all, humans first.

"At the heart of education is the relationship between teachers and students." — Sir Ken Robinson

1

Preparing Your Classroom for Literacy Instruction

"Make the environment as important as the curriculum and the two support each other during instruction." — Lesley Mandel Morrow

When we are given our teaching assignment for the year, there is much to consider! What do we know about students of this age: their interests, their skills, their development? What do we know about the curriculum in the grade level we've been assigned? What resources are available for the various disciplines of study? What school supplies will students bring on the first day? From broader questions to minute details, the queries are many.

In *Imagine If…*, Sir Ken Robinson and Kate Robinson (2022) suggest that "A physical environment is more than cosmetic, it affects the mood, motivation, and vitality of the whole school community." (78)

Another consideration is the classroom environment. For some, it is the starting point—until the classroom is set up, they can't possibly begin to plan. For others, classroom set-up may be an afterthought. And yet, our classroom environment plays a significant role in literacy learning and the acquisition of literacy behaviors. A well-planned classroom can truly support our students' learning while making it easier for us to meet our overall goals. Time spent establishing an environment for optimal learning up front will save us time throughout the year—in itself a good reason to be intentional about setting up our classrooms with literacy learning in mind.

As a writer-in-residence, I work with teachers in many schools. One thing has become abundantly clear: not all classrooms are created equal. In some schools, the classrooms are spacious and designed with ample room to delineate various sections within the class. In others, space is minimal, desks are crowded, and teachers are doing the best they can with what they've got. When configuring your classroom, consider how you might have to adapt the sections of the classroom discussed in this chapter to make them work in your space.

The Big Picture

In her book *The Heart-Centered Teacher*, Regie Routman (2024) says, "our immediate environment influences how well we learn, feel part of a community, take risks, and thrive—or not" (92).

When considering the set-up of your classroom, consider both functionality and feel. You—and your students—will spend almost 200 days of the year within those four walls: make it an inviting and enjoyable place to be! The classroom space should also be practical and include a set-up convenient for collaboration and discussion, easy access to classroom books, and desks or table space with organized materials to maximize instructional time. Let's break it down…

Desk or Table Arrangement

Throughout this book, and especially in Chapters 2 and 4, you will find many ways to leverage oral language to help students articulate their thinking and construct meaning from the concepts being taught. With this in mind, consider how students are sitting. If your students sit in pairs or in small groups at tables, the arrangement is already conducive for talk and collaboration. If your students have individual desks, how might you arrange them for ease of collaboration? Pods of four, or four desks in an L-shape, tend to be convenient for both individual work when necessary and easy collaboration with a partner or group. If that isn't feasible, another option is paired desks in rows. Whenever possible, we want to avoid isolating students in individual rows.

Silent classrooms are relics of the past. Yes, there are times students will be working quietly and independently, but often, we want to engage them in turn-and-talk opportunities: either with a partner or a small group. Students shouldn't have to move to make this happen. Opportunities for talk, collaboration, and meaningful conversation should be built into the day. If students have to physically move every time we want them to turn-and-talk, we're losing valuable instructional time. There is also the danger that we may avoid conversation or collaboration if it cannot happen quickly and efficiently.

When deciding on the arrangement of desks or tables, also consider where students will keep their supplies. If your students have desks with storage, perhaps the decision is made for you. If your students will be working at tables, consider various storage options such as bins, magazine file holders, and pencil boxes. Keep in mind students will likely bring school supplies for the entire year, but it can be cumbersome to keep everything they bring in their desk or bin. Consider using a large, plastic resealable bag to store extra supplies: one for each student. The more organized you are, the more organized your students are likely to be. The inverse is also true.

A Classroom Library

Classroom libraries are essential in all elementary classrooms, regardless of grade level. You may be fortunate and find yourself in a classroom with one already in place, at least partially. In some schools, the parent council contributes financially to stocking and maintaining classroom libraries. However, for many teachers a classroom library is a personal book collection accumulated over time. If you do find yourself building your own, there are many options to make it more affordable. Book clubs—such as Scholastic—provide inexpensive options, often with book sets, to enable teachers to add to their classroom libraries. The site BookOutlet.ca also has books at discounted prices. Many of the books in our classroom libraries are softcover, which also helps keep costs down.

The books in our classroom libraries should be available at a variety of levels to support students reading below grade level and to challenge those reading above grade level. We also need to ensure there are a variety of genres. Students should have access to picture books, early chapter books, novels, and graphic novels—a wide array of text forms helps ensure we capture the interest of all. When considering fiction, be sure to include categories such as realistic fiction,

"Fostering conversations that matter requires a classroom and school culture of respectful and trusting relationships" (Routman 2024, 52).

This reference to a wide variety of levels is not a reference to *levelled books,* which will be discussed in the upcoming pages.

fantasy, and mystery. When considering nonfiction, expand beyond traditional nonfiction to include biographies, autobiographies, memoirs, dictionaries, picture dictionaries, and cookbooks. Librarians and booksellers are happy to provide specific recommendations. Also look for award-winning books to round out your collection. As an example, the Young Reader's Choice Awards (YRCA) are a great reference. Young readers in Alaska, Alberta, British Columbia, Idaho, Montana, and Washington choose both the nominated books and the winners. Other provinces, too, have book lists chosen by young readers. And remember, the books should be as diverse as our students, representing authors and characters of many cultural backgrounds.

Be sure to include magazines in your classroom library as well. Consider these selections that have options available for a variety of age groups, including our youngest in Kindergarten: *Highlights*, *National Geographic Kids*, and *Owl Magazine*. If you are a parent, perhaps you have a magazine subscription for your own children. You can bring in the back issues as your children finish with them. If not, check with your administration or parent council to see if this is something that might be funded.

I realized the importance of having varied and diverse reading materials when—for some reason—I brought my car manual into the classroom. I think I had to make an appointment and the contact information was within the manual. Whatever the reason, a student noticed the manual on my desk and asked excitedly, "Can I read this?" Let me tell you: I have never read a car manual from cover to cover and I never will. I have read the odd page here or there if—and only if—I needed to. This student read my car manual for *days*. He devoured it, in fact. This experience reminded me that I needed to expand the types of text and topics in my classroom library. Something I would never choose to read was fascinating to this student. We shouldn't stock our libraries according to our interests alone.

Ideally, we want students to be able to take classroom library books home to read in addition to reading them during class time. Some teachers are hesitant about this, especially if it is their personal collection and they are concerned books will not be returned. I look at it like this: if a student takes a book home and it doesn't find its way back, I hope it is being enjoyed wherever it is. For me, the possible benefits outweigh the risk. And, typically, if you demonstrate care for books—or *book love* as the case may be—your students will as well.

What does your classroom library look like? Ideally, the books should be easily accessible to students, with the covers of books visible rather than only the spines. Few have been inspired to read a book based on its spine alone! Housing your books in baskets or bins is ideal. The books may then be sorted by genre, topic, or alphabetically by author's name. Sometimes, books by a popular author like Robert Munsch or Gordon Korman will fill an entire basket. Whichever method you choose, be intentional. Include labels on the baskets or bins to make it easy for students to find books they might enjoy.

Keep in mind we don't want the baskets so full it becomes difficult to flip through and see what's inside. We also want to make the organization system easy for students so they can return books to their proper spot. Consider enlisting the help of student volunteers who could be responsible for a weekly tidy and re-organization of the library. This is a wonderful way to nurture our students' love of books, too—those who may already feel passionate about books, or those who need some nudging.

If you store your books on a bookshelf, without baskets or bins, be sure to display some on top of the shelves, and change the display regularly. This often

When we create our classroom libraries, we are ultimately giving our students exposure and permission to read a wide variety of text.

Suggestions for engaging students in independent reading will be addressed in Chapters 3 and 6.

In addition to books for the classroom library, I have a large personal collection of picture books, often hardcover. These I typically store in my teacher space so that I can share them with students as mentor texts or read them aloud during a unit in another curricular area. Often, I prefer if students don't see these in advance of the lesson. (Much more about mentor texts in Chapter 7.)

motivates students, or prompts them to choose the featured books. Are you studying magnets, space, or rocks and minerals in science? Then you know what's on display! Is it April, National Poetry Month? Or are you studying the work of a particular author? Be intentional about what is displayed at various times of the year, showcasing both fiction and nonfiction whenever you can. Not only will the books on display entice your students, you will also expose them to related vocabulary and background information.

As an example, if you are teaching the element of color during art class, display a variety of books connected to this topic: *Color Blocked* by Ashley Sorenson, *The Day the Crayons Quit* by Drew Daywalt, *Green* by Laura Vaccaro Seeger, *Mixed: A Colorful Story* by Arree Chung, *Mix it Up!* by Herve Tullet, *National Geographic: Animals That Change Color* by Libby Romero, and *One* by Kathryn Otoshi. Adding a book such as *The Arts: A Visual Encyclopedia* by DK Publishing may also put the element of color in context for budding artists. There are also books—especially for primary students—that connect color to feelings. You might decide to put some of these on the shelf too: *The Color Monster: A Story About Emotions* by Anna Llenas and *My Many Colored Days* by Dr. Seuss. A diverse display of books on a connected topic will help ensure all students find something of interest and often leads to interesting discussions.

Levelled books—yes or no?

You may be aware of the debate over levelled books in recent years. Fountas and Pinnell introduced the F&P Text Level Gradient in 1996. This levelling system is often referred to as F&P Levels or Guided Reading Levels. The levels were designed to help teachers provide text appropriate for student readers: not so difficult that they become frustrated but not so easy that they are not practicing skills. Many schools latched onto this idea and created bins full of levelled books. In addition, many teachers were asked to assess the reading levels of their students, often multiple times per year.

A few problems arose. First with assessments. The benchmark assessment designed to determine student reading levels—especially with older students—takes quite some time. Many teachers were directed to use instructional time for assessment: hours when they could have been teaching were instead used to determine reading levels, one student at a time. Sometimes, the collected data was submitted to the district or school without teachers using it to inform instruction or change their practices with students.

A second problem: reading levels were often shared with parents, sometimes on report cards. While at first this might not seem problematic, it became a contentious issue in many school districts. If students didn't appear to be improving either within a grade or from grade to grade, parents grew concerned and began to question teachers and administrators. However, if teachers were not administering assessments in precisely the same way, these discrepancies may have affected results and then been misleading. There were often other factors—factors parents were not aware of—contributing to the students' reported reading levels.

A third concern: students were sometimes told they could only read levelled books (no others) and only from one bin. Some students began to identify themselves as 'a level G reader,' for example, and were reluctant to read or try anything else.

After much controversy about levelled texts in recent years, Fountas and Pinnell have reiterated that the levels were designed to help teachers make good decisions for instruction and that they are not to be used as labels for students.

Can we continue to use levelled books in our classrooms? We certainly can. Levelled books help ensure students are successful and are practicing the skills we teach. The caution is this: the levels can stifle students if we're not careful about how they are approached. It is essential that we provide time when students can read any book on our classroom shelves! This will ultimately lead to greater engagement and joy in reading. Even if a student reads a portion of a book and then decides not to continue, that's okay! Perhaps a student chooses a book about sharks that is above their independent level: if there is high engagement, they will push through and read what they can. That's okay, too. Keep in mind some students may choose levelled books during independent reading if they feel more successful with them. Choice is key, and students should have the option to choose whatever topic or genre they desire.

In *Disrupting Thinking*, Kylene Beers and Robert Probst (2017) suggest this approach:

> We have kids read at their instructional level when we are instructing, when we have taught a skill that we want them to practice immediately. If we're in a school that uses guided reading, then during the guided reading time with a small group, of course those students will be reading a text at their instructional level. (138)

In other words, let students choose any book from the classroom library during independent reading, but when students are practicing skills during whole-class or small-group instruction, use books written at students' instructional levels.

A Reading Corner

Picture books should be used in all elementary classrooms regardless of grade! Remember, as the teacher, you create the norms in your classroom. If you regularly use picture books as mentor texts during mini-lessons or to connect with content-area curriculum, your students will understand their usefulness and not question their use at all.

Whenever possible—and no matter the grade level—I incorporate a reading corner near our classroom library. Throughout the day, we gather for read-alouds and also for independent or paired reading opportunities. In primary classrooms, it is relatively easy to ensure that the reading corner is a comfortable space that accommodates all students. Both the desks and students are smaller, after all! In upper elementary classrooms, where both the furniture and students are larger, it may be more challenging to create a space where everyone can gather. But if you have the room, do it! There is nothing better than gathering students—even in upper elementary—to share a picture book. Doing so from the front of the class is fine, but it is much more effective for student engagement when we can sit in close proximity. If you don't have enough space for everyone to gather at once, consider how you can still create a reading environment near the classroom library where students can choose to read independently.

One additional note about reading corners: if you do have one, capitalize on the physical transition from desks to reading corner (and eventually back again) as a built-in movement or stretch break. This can be a natural, embedded opportunity to refresh many of our students.

Space for Small-Group Work

Effective classroom environments typically include a table where you can work with a small group of students at a time. Often, this will be for guided reading (more on this topic in Chapter 6), but the space can be used for a variety of purposes throughout the day. For instance, you can work with a small group who needs additional support when the majority of the class is working independently or in partners. This space in your classroom is the ideal place to bring them together. Or, if a small group of students are working together on a project—in science or health or social studies—perhaps they choose to work in this space.

One caution: in some classrooms, an additional table becomes storage. Do your best to keep it clear to be used for and with students.

Literacy Stations

As part of the discussion on planning in Chapter 3, you will be encouraged to develop literacy stations to reinforce the literacy learning taking place. Because space is often limited, and for maximum flexibility, I tend to store my literacy stations in bins of various sizes. Students are then directed to take a bin from the shelf (or a large zippered bag from within the bin) and find a space to work with their partner or small group. When planning your classroom space, you may want to set aside a bookshelf for these literacy station bins.

Bulletin Boards and Wall Space

Although you want your classroom to look appealing when the students (and perhaps their parents) walk in on the first day of school, do not have everything already "up." Doing so ensures that whatever is on your walls becomes wallpaper: students tend not to notice what's there beyond the first impression. The foundations of our bulletin boards can be in place, the titles or labels, for example, but most of the content will be added *with* students as part of our instruction. So how do we prepare the wall space for what's to come? What should we plan to put on our bulletin boards? There are a few key sections to consider: an alphabet frieze, a word wall, a calendar space, a morning message, a sound wall, a morpheme wall, and room for posters and anchor charts. Some teachers also designate space for content curriculum. As you read through these sections, notice that some bulletin boards are appropriate for all classrooms, some are specifically used in primary, and others are most applicable in upper elementary.

Alphabet Frieze

As you know, English is written with a Latin-script alphabet consisting of 26 letters. These letters can each be written in two forms: uppercase and lowercase. Although we can easily recognize and name these letters, we can't underestimate the challenge for our youngest learners or those new to the language. If you learned English as an adult, or if you have you ever learned a language with an alphabet or symbols different from the English alphabet, you understand the complexity: recognizing each symbol, learning to write each symbol with proper formation, and understanding the sounds attached (or the meaning, as in a language such as Mandarin). An alphabet frieze—often posted above a bulletin board or whiteboard—is an essential reference tool for our students. The most effective will include a picture of an object beginning with the letter and both the upper and lowercase forms of the letters ideally shown on tri-lined paper. (Tri-lined paper has a bold line at the top and the bottom, but also a dotted line in the middle. This supports students with proper letter formation.)

I also recommend students each have an alphabet on their desks or tables, especially in Kindergarten, Grade 1, and Grade 2. For some, looking up to the wall is one step too many. The easy reference tool on each desk—often on a nameplate—will be used regularly. Not providing students with these essential instructional tools is a disservice, making an already challenging task more challenging.

If you teach Grade 3 and above, consider your individual students. Are there students in your class who might benefit from having easy access to a printed alphabet? If your students are required to learn cursive writing, find both an alphabet frieze for your wall and nameplates for students that include letters written in cursive.

Word Walls

After the alphabet frieze, word walls are perhaps the most useful reference tool that we can include on our classroom walls for literacy learning—when used deliberately. In fact, I encourage teachers of all grade levels to use a word wall, even moving into our junior high and senior high classrooms. Obviously, the appearance and content will differ according to the grade level we teach, but it is a powerful tool for students of all ages.

One day in late August—just days before the school year was to begin—I was presenting a session to teachers at a Kindergarten to Grade 4 school. In our discussion about word walls, I reminded teachers of the importance of building the word wall *with* students, adding words together throughout the year. After the session was over, one of the teachers came up and asked: "Did you see my classroom… is that why you said that?"

I reassured her that, no, not at all—this is something I say in every session I give on the topic. Our exchange continued something like this:

"I'm going to go take down all of the words from my word wall right now!"

"I'm sorry. My intent was not to give you more work before the year starts!"

"Oh no! It makes so much sense. I don't want my word wall to become wallpaper!"

In our elementary classrooms, the word wall will probably take up more room than most other things. A word wall on a 4' x 8' or 4' x 6' bulletin board is not difficult to fill as the year goes on. Choose a prime, highly visible location for your word wall. If used properly, students will refer to it often. When you set up your word wall, put up only the letters, not the words. Be sure to plan ahead before placing the letters. Typically, more space is needed for words that begin letters such as *h, s, t,* and *w.* Letters such as *q, x,* and *z* will usually not require a large space as not many **high-frequency words** begin with these letters.

In addition to adding high-frequency words each week, you might also incorporate Tier Two vocabulary. These are words that are used in academic contexts and that cross disciplinary boundaries because they are used in many subject areas. Words like *analyze, describe,* and *explain,* are Tier Two words. They are

If you choose to maintain flexible seating in your classroom and do not use nameplates, consider how you can still include an alphabet at each working space. If your custodian is concerned about nameplates being taped to work spaces, there are many ways of working around this issue.

The use of word walls, sound walls, and morpheme walls will be explained more fully in Chapter 5: Word Study. If you only have room for one, make it a word wall and make it intentional.

As the details of our classroom environment are discussed, you may encounter unfamiliar terminology. See the glossary on page 159 for words in bold print. Further explanation of the terms and concepts will be provided in later chapters.

The Three Tiers of Vocabulary will be discussed in Chapter 5.

helpful for all students, but in upper elementary in particular, you may want to draw special attention to them. Although we will discuss how to teach Tier Two vocabulary in a later chapter, I mention them here because you may want to consider how to incorporate them on your word wall. Some teachers choose to color-code them, for example.

Although it may be tempting to create a *digital* word wall and display it on your interactive whiteboard when students are writing, students will not have easy access to this digital reference throughout the day. Ideally, it should be something visible at all times, not only during structured writing time.

If you do not have bulletin board space available for a word wall, you may have to get creative. I have seen teachers use the front of cabinet doors, or find space under a whiteboard. Another possibility is to provide students with file folders in which they create personal word walls. These folders can be prepped ahead of time, with the letters already in place on the inside of the folders. Then, throughout the year, students can add words as you discuss them each week. One disadvantage of the file folders if they are the only method used: it becomes difficult for us as teachers to refer to the word wall on a regular basis. Also, out of sight sometimes means out of mind. For teachers *and* students.

Calendar Space

In our Kindergarten and primary classrooms, we often begin the day with the routine of *calendar*. This morning routine reinforces Tier One vocabulary, as well as concepts in both our language arts and mathematics curricula. During calendar time, we talk about the day, the month, the year, and we likely add the date to a physical calendar. It can also be effective to track the number of days we are in school with straws or popsicle sticks, making groups of ten as we go. In my primary classes, I had three plastic cups labelled *hundreds*, *tens*, and *ones*. As a class, each day we would add a straw to the *ones* cup and change the number on the cup accordingly. On a day there were ten *ones*, we created a bundle of ten by adding an elastic and then put it in the *tens* cup. We then changed the number on the *ones* cup to a zero and added a one to the *tens* cup. This is a highly visible lesson in place value, especially effective as it will be repeated throughout the year. Although this example is math-related, this routine creates many opportunities for oral language practice and exposes students to important vocabulary. Whatever you decide your calendar time is going to entail, think through what you need in the space beforehand.

A Morning Message

A morning message is an excellent way to create meaningful text for students that incorporates recent learning and gives them an opportunity to practice their phonetic knowledge. (More on this in Chapter 5.)

Often adjacent to calendar time—either before or after—students can engage in a shared reading of a morning message, written by you prior to students entering the classroom each day. I have included this section here as something to keep in mind when creating your space. If you choose to write your morning message on your interactive whiteboard (ahead of the students' arrival), you may not need to consider the classroom space. However, if you decide to write the message on a whiteboard easel or chart paper, for example, this is something to include in or near your reading corner. I highly recommend the use of a morning message in all primary classrooms, and I have seen many teachers in upper elementary use them effectively too.

Sound Walls

When I began my teaching career, I found myself replacing a Grade 1 teacher partway into the school year. I was fortunate to learn from what she had already established in her classroom and—because it was a fairly big school—I also had grade-level colleagues. Every Grade 1 and Grade 2 classroom in the school had a large wall space dedicated to a sound wall known as Sound City. Sound City is based on the work of Anna Ingham from her book *The Blended Sound-Sight Program of Learning*. I found her method and philosophy powerful. At the time, I was simply doing what I saw others doing. When I was working on my Masters of Education in literacy instruction, I understood why her method has been so successful over so many decades: it includes explicit, systematic instruction in both **phonological awareness** and **phonics**.

In recent years, there has been a resurgence in sound walls in our Grade 1 and Grade 2 classrooms in particular. This is due to the **Science of Reading** (SoR) research related to phonological awareness and phonics during the past few decades. Although I do occasionally encounter Sound City in my work with teachers across the country, the sound walls used most often today look considerably different. Most have two main sections: vowel valley and consonants. Many include what are known as **articulatory gestures**: what the mouth, lips, and tongue are doing to produce a particular sound. If you teach Grades 1 or 2 and plan on using a sound wall, look to the resource you are using to determine the amount of wall space you will need.

I highly recommend taking an in-service or session on sound walls if you plan to use one with students. I have encountered some teachers with sound walls who have bravely admitted, "I don't know how to use it." Why have it if it will not be used? We run the risk of creating more wallpaper…

Morpheme Walls

Research supports the explicit teaching of **morphology** to support our students in many areas of language learning: reading, writing, vocabulary development, and understanding the structure of words. Morphology is the study of **morphemes**—the smallest units of meaning in a word. Prefixes, base elements (bases and roots), and suffixes are all morphemes. Preparing a morpheme wall with these headings—prefixes, roots, suffixes—will be useful for the study of morphology throughout the year. Although primary students learn basic morphology, especially some simple prefixes and suffixes, a morpheme wall might not be as necessary in these classrooms. However, if you teach Grade 3 or higher, I recommend finding the space. It certainly won't be as large as your word wall, but it will support students with this aspect of word study. As you teach specific morphemes throughout the year, you can add a card under the appropriate heading which shows the morpheme, its meaning, and perhaps some example words. (More about the teaching of morphology in Chapter 5.)

Posters vs. Anchor Charts

Some teachers feel the need to *fill* the wall space of their classrooms before students arrive at the beginning of the year. Keep in mind that it is much more effective to put things up as we introduce or teach a concept. You may be tempted to put up posters to fill space. Perhaps a few with messages such as growth mindset or a positive attitude are suitable. However, with effective literacy learning in mind, we want to ensure that we have room for **anchor charts** as we create them with our students throughout the year.

What is an anchor chart?

Even though an anchor chart is created with students present, some preplanning is recommended (a framework, headings, or related visuals, for example) to ensure it becomes an effective visual reference.

An anchor chart is a tool used to support our instruction and "anchor" the learning for our students. Typically, teachers use a large sheet of chart paper on an easel or A-frame stand: the page can then be removed and posted somewhere visible after its creation. Anchor charts are often co-constructed with students, or, at the very least, created in front of students. The purpose is to capture the concept or strategy being taught in both words and visuals. When we create the anchor charts *with* students and they then see us physically adding it to the wall, it becomes much more meaningful and they are more likely to use it for future reference. Not only will they realize it's there, they will know *why* it's there and *how* to use it.

For added effectiveness, you may ask students to create a personal anchor chart to mimic your own and personalize it to support their own learning. A large coil-bound book with blank pages is ideal for this purpose—a visual journal, for example. By adding adhesive tabs to create sections, visual journals can be used to capture students' literacy learning (*My Literacy Notebook*) or used across subject areas (*My Visual Journal* or *My Learning Notebook*).

Content Curriculum

You may choose to reserve some of your wall space for other areas of the curriculum. Use it to display content specific to the concepts you are teaching, or to highlight student work. Often, these content-area bulletin boards connect to literacy as well. In science, for example, you may choose to create a *wonder wall*, where students add a speech bubble with their wonderings about an area of study. Or, you may choose to post visual representations of vocabulary words in mathematics or social studies. The options are many: be creative! If you decide to display student work, this can be a way to honor the effort students have made, instill a sense of pride, and provide examples of excellent products or alternative approaches.

Classroom Labels

Your school division may use the term English Language Learners where others use Multilingual Learners. By definition, Multilingual Learners are students who are developing skills in multiple languages; this includes students learning English as an additional language.

Another important consideration for your physical space is the use of labels. Imagine suddenly finding yourself in a classroom where a language other than English is spoken, where you don't know the names of anything around you. This everyday vocabulary is considered Tier One vocabulary. If I were in a classroom with an unfamiliar language, I'd appreciate labels. It's one thing to hear the language, but it's a whole other thing to *see* it and eventually *say* it. For primary classrooms, and in classrooms where there are Level 1 or 2 English Language Learners or Multilingual Learners, consider displaying labels for everyday objects and places within your classroom: desk, table, chair, window, door, classroom library, etc. If you are concerned that it looks too primary for your upper elementary classroom, all that is required is a simple conversation with students. When we explain our reasoning, students tend to immediately understand and often begin to support their peers with this vocabulary. And, keep in mind, the labels don't have to be large and conspicuous, but having them available is a powerful tool for students who are learning this essential vocabulary.

Several reproducibles with common classroom vocabulary words are provided for your convenience at the end of this chapter. You may choose to print and laminate the labels to put up around your classroom. To assist with organization, some of the labels (crayons, erasers, glue, markers, pencils) could be placed on bins storing collective school supplies.

As you set up your class for the first time, or as you refresh your current set-up, take yourself on a field trip to other classrooms. Talk to your colleagues about the intentionality of their classroom environment and the role of literacy in the spaces created for students. Remember there are many considerations, but all are connected to functionality and feel. Be intentional.

Classroom Labels

backpack	bookshelf
bulletin board	chair
classroom	classroom library
clock	computer
crayons	desk
door	erasers
garbage	glue
hallway	hole punch

Pembroke Publishers ©2025 *Literacy Instruction Matters* by Karen Filewych ISBN 978-1-55138-371-2

Classroom Labels

literacy stations	lunch kit
map	markers
pencil crayons	pencil sharpener
pencils	pens
reading corner	recycling
rulers	scissors
stapler	table
whiteboard	window

Pembroke Publishers ©2025 *Literacy Instruction Matters* by Karen Filewych ISBN 978-1-55138-371-2

2

The Role of Language in Our Classrooms

"Teaching is listening, learning is talking." — Deborah Meier

The above quotation might at first seem contrary to our view of teaching. Teaching is *listening*? When we conjure an image of a teacher or think about what we do each day, we likely envision the teacher talking. This quote is a reminder that our students need to be talking too: it is, arguably, when they learn the most. In fact, we should be intentional about leveraging all aspects of language to enhance student learning throughout the curriculum.

The Nature of Language

During professional development sessions, I often ask educators these questions: *Why do we use language? What is the function of language?* The first answer is inevitably the same: communication. This answer certainly isn't wrong, but it is revealing. We do use language to communicate but its function is much more than communication. The front matter of the Alberta Language Arts and Literature curriculum (2022) says, "Language is a uniquely structured system that forms the basis for thinking, communicating, and learning." It is essential that we intentionally engage all three of these functions of language in our classrooms. We *communicate* through language, yes, but we also *think* and *learn* through language.

Language and literacy underpin all we do. Imagine going through your day without language. Without reading. Without speaking. Without listening. Imagine your classroom—in any subject area—without language. It's difficult to do.

Language is divided into two main categories: receptive and expressive. *Receptive language* includes listening, reading, and viewing. *Expressive language* includes speaking, writing, and representing. But all of these skills—often called strands—are inexplicably intertwined and frequently written in pairs: listening and speaking, reading and writing, viewing and representing.

The Six Strands of Language

listening and **speaking**

reading and **writing**

viewing and **representing**

receptive language   expressive language

Language arts is a skill- or process-based curriculum. Many of the other subjects are content- or topic-based. The beauty of integration is that students can be exposed to concepts and vocabulary from content-based subjects while practicing the skills or processes that we teach in language arts. Breaking free from the silos of subject areas is an efficient use of our time and often brings relevance to student learning.

Think about how these strands are at work in our classrooms every day—and not just in language arts. During every lesson you teach, language is at work. You may be speaking and your students listening. Your students may be speaking and you and their peers listening. How about reading? In how many contexts throughout the day are we or our students reading? We know reading is not exclusive to language arts. It is something our students are doing—should be doing—in all subject areas. One early mistake I made as an elementary teacher was not being more intentional about integration. I didn't capitalize on the fact that I was teaching most subjects to my students. My lessons were quite isolated into the various subject areas. It didn't occur to me to use the science text to reinforce a reading strategy. If I did, it was incidental and not as intentional as it should have been. Imagine the difference if we deliberately capitalize on the nature of language to enhance learning in all areas of study.

The Strands of Listening and Speaking

When considering the strands of language, Thomas Newkirk (2023) suggests:

> Oral language—talk and listening comprehension—is innate. We are biologically predisposed to learn it. We accomplish mastery with lightning speed in childhood. The print counterparts—writing and reading—are not innate; they are learned. Print is too recent an evolutionary development for humans to automatically have mastery over it. We need to be taught to read and write. (1)

If you have been around a toddler or preschooler, you have experienced the "lightning speed" Newkirk speaks about. How it is that children acquire oral language at such an incredible rate—hearing words and then using them themselves, first as individual words and then, before long, stringing short sentences together? As teachers, we should consider how to capitalize on our students' innate abilities with oral language to support them with their overall learning.

In my roles as both language arts consultant and administrator, I had the pleasure of observing many teachers at work in their classrooms. I was often impressed with the creativity of the lessons and the rapport teachers establish with their students. There was one thing, however, that I noticed quite often, even with excellent, experienced teachers. When asking their class a question following instruction or a demonstration, many teachers immediately chose the first or second student who raised a hand. I'm sure I've often done the same.

Consider your own class. How many students typically raise their hands to answer questions? Most teachers say between three and five. And which students? You can likely name them as they are often the same individuals regardless of subject area. Herein lies the problem. When we ask a question, we shouldn't want one answer from one student. One answer from one student does not indicate that our class understands the concept; it simply shows that one student understands. The point of the question should be to engage *all* students in *thinking* about the question and the content. By choosing the first raised hand, we are not giving the rest of the class time to think about the answer, never mind the chance to respond. Besides, students are smart. If they notice that three or four of their peers always answer, they check out. Not only do they not have to answer, they don't even have to think about the question: they're off the hook, so to speak.

If we keep in mind that students *think* and *learn* through language, we must find ways to ensure *all students* are thinking and talking about the content, ultimately leading to better understanding. Thankfully, some small shifts in practice can make this a reality. To begin, we can give more wait time after we ask a question. Then, we direct all students to turn-and-talk about the question with a partner. What are students doing in these moments? Constructing meaning… articulating their thinking… practicing conventions of language and communication… sharing opinions and justifying their answers. When we do bring them back for the whole-class discussion, more students—more than those three to five that first came to mind—are likely to answer. Since they've now all had an opportunity to talk things through, think about their learning, and make connections to their own lives, students may feel more comfortable sharing with the larger group. Even better, all students have been engaged in the learning process. In their book *Making Thinking Visible*, Ritchhart, Church, and Morrison (2011) explain:

> We need to make thinking visible because it provides us with the information we as teachers need to plan opportunities that will take students' learning to the next level and enable continued engagement with the ideas being explored. It is only when we understand what our students are thinking, feeling, and attending to that we can use that knowledge to further engage and support them in the process of understanding. (27)

Not only then is the process of turn-and-talk helping students learn, it also provides us teachers with valuable information.

Does the turn-and-talk take more time? It does. But it is certainly time well spent. Sometimes, as teachers, it is easy to get caught up thinking about all we have to cover and we move quickly through content. One correct answer by one student might reassure us that students have understood. But it is essential that we ensure *all* students have the opportunity to engage and think and talk about whatever it is we are teaching. Not one. Not five. All.

When should we use this turn-and-talk strategy? Throughout the day in all subject areas! We can use it to activate prior knowledge, after a portion of material has been taught, after a shared reading, or after "doing" something such as an experiment or an activity. This simple strategy will ensure students are talking to learn.

Create a signal, cue, or phrase that you will use to bring students back from their turn-and-talk interactions. The consistency of a routine will assist with classroom management and ensure maximum time on task.

Realizing the power of the turn-and-talk strategy—and how often we should be using it—we see the importance of the arrangement of desks discussed in Chapter 1. Asking students to turn-and-talk should be quick and convenient.

Meaningful Talk

If you've taught for a few years, you've likely had a class of talkers! That chatty class who rarely provide a moment of quiet. Although they might be talking, when it comes to learning, student talk should be meaningful. You may be familiar with John Hattie's work on *visible learning*. Hattie and his team study various effects on learning, classroom discourse being one. In *Teaching Literacy in the Visible Learning Classroom*, Fisher, Frey, and Hattie (2017) reference Hattie's research:

> Let's consider increasing classroom discourse (synonymous with classroom discussion or dialogue). Students would be invited to talk with their peers in collaborative groups, working to solve complex and rich tasks…. The effect size of classroom discourse is 0.82, well above our threshold, and likely to result in two years of learning gains for a year of schooling. (3)

They consider this effect size to be in the high range, indicating that meaningful talk is a powerful practice in our classrooms. In order to create meaningful talk, we have to ask meaningful questions. In Chapter 4: Oral Language, we will spend more time considering the types of questions we are asking.

> Many years ago, a colleague and I took the time to observe each other while teaching. We each gave the other something to watch for. This was not about the content. It was about our methods, our tendencies. Afterwards, we simply talked about our observations. This was one of the most enlightening experiences I have had as a teacher. We don't often take the time or the opportunity to reflect on our own practice. I learned new strategies from this teacher but I also learned a lot about myself. Think about a colleague you trust. Would you be open to having them observe a lesson and watch for the amount of student participation and your tendencies when questioning?

The Strands of Reading and Writing

The strands of reading and writing build on the strands of listening and speaking. Unlike oral language, which is considered innate, reading and writing are learned and therefore require more explicit instruction.

Reading with Intention

When it comes to reading, research shows how important it is that students engage in reading during the school day. Unfortunately, if they are not reading with us, they're not likely reading without us. For this reason—and many others— elementary teachers often embed time spent reading into the daily schedule. Some of this reading will occur during language arts but some should occur in other subjects too. Consider what reading might look like during a science lesson at the beginning of a unit on magnetism. Surround students with a variety of books about magnets. While they are reading, give them each a sticky note or two. Perhaps they write a *wondering* about what they're reading, a *question*, or

Although reading with intention is effective, remember that there should also be time when students are reading and enjoying whatever they choose without a task given by the teacher! Balance is key. (More on this in Chapters 3 and 6.)

an *unfamiliar vocabulary word*—whatever you decide for that day. This reading becomes more intentional in a few ways. Yes, they're reading, which is in itself a necessary skill to practice, but they are also gaining background knowledge for the topic being studied, being exposed to new vocabulary, and beginning to think about related ideas.

Another way to demonstrate reading with intention: model the practice of rereading text with students: instructions, information, anything! Some of our students presume that if they have to reread something, they must be a poor reader. I want my students to understand that rereading is a strategy used by effective readers.

Writing as a Form of Thinking

When I began teaching, I didn't give enough thought to how I might leverage language to help students understand what it was I was teaching. I certainly didn't use writing in the ways I do today. If you know my previous books, you may be familiar with my work on freewriting, inspired by Peter Elbow. My first book, *How Do I Get Them to Write?*, has a chapter on freewriting. The positive response from teachers led to my second book, *Freewriting with Purpose*, which is entirely focused on how to use freewriting effectively in our classrooms. When I first introduced this process to students, my intention was to break down the barriers and reluctance to writing. As I detail in both of the books mentioned above, I discovered many other benefits to using this form of writing in the classroom. One of the most important benefits? Writing as a form of thinking. Just like talking, freewriting is another way of giving all students an opportunity to engage in the content: thinking through their learning and articulating connections and questions. As is evident, this form of writing is more about process and less about end product.

One day, after freewriting with my Grade 6 class, we were all reading our work quietly to ourselves. Suddenly one of my students blurted, "I didn't know I thought that!" His exclamation was a reminder that writing, truly, is a form of thinking. Why save writing for the language arts classroom? Perhaps our language arts time is when we teach students the *skills* involved in writing. But writing itself… why not embed it into science or social studies, health or music? The intent of freewriting in other subject areas is not for the writing to be submitted and assessed: it is meant as thinking on the page. The focus is on the process and not the end product. If students worry that their writing will be read and assessed by the teacher, the stakes, the anxiety, and often the reluctance rise dramatically. This low-stakes writing—writing not to be handed in or assessed—is another way to leverage language to support student learning. (More on freewriting in Chapter 7.)

The Strands of Viewing and Representing

Consider the visual nature of today's society and the amount of time this generation spends looking at a screen. Our students are constantly bombarded with images, graphics, animations, and videos. And really, the definition of "text" is perpetually expanding with changing technologies. Our students are *viewing* messages continually—messages in different formats and styles, with different biases and intents. It is more essential than ever that our students become discerning, critical-thinking viewers of information. In fact, it's a matter of safety.

Our curricular documents in language arts often outline the various text forms our students should be exposed to. Regardless of the form, it is important that we discuss the words, the visuals, and the creator's intentions. The strand of viewing should occur throughout the day in various subject areas: capitalize on each opportunity that arises, again making discussions more relevant.

Viewing is one of the receptive strands of language learning. And what about its opposite, the expressive strand of representing? This too, can be embedded throughout our lessons in all subject areas. We tend to ask students to express themselves primarily through words. But how might we ask our students to represent their thinking through other forms such as charts, diagrams, movements, gestures, sounds, models, images, posters, video presentations, dramatizations, or music. It's incredible to see what students create when they are given choice in how to represent their thinking. A change in form often leads to creativity and innovation. Understandably, some forms will be more appropriate in certain situations or within particular timeframes, but this strand should certainly not be neglected. When I look ahead to potential careers our current students may consider, the strands of viewing and representing seem even more relevant!

The strand of representing doesn't have to be time-consuming or complex. Sometimes we might simply say, *"Use pictures and words to demonstrate your understanding of today's lesson."* Given this task, student work will vary: some students might draw and label a diagram, some might create something metaphorical, some might create a visual equation. It may be necessary to remind them there is not one right way to represent their thinking: they can choose what works for them. The more opportunities they have to represent their thinking, the more confident they become.

Take the time now to think of a recent lesson you've taught—in a subject other than language arts. What did you like about the lesson? Why do you think that particular lesson came to mind? Now consider how you might improve the lesson if you were to teach it again tomorrow. How could you leverage various strands of language to improve student learning and increase participation?

Let Students in on the Secret

Have you ever been in the middle of a lesson and heard the question, "Why do we need to know this?" If you haven't heard it yet, be prepared, it will come. At some point, some student will voice this exact sentiment. What I love about teaching language arts is that we know our students will use the skills every day of their lives. And I want my students to know that too! Beers and Probst (2017) suggest this about students: "When they discover the relevance, their energy for and attention to the task will soar. Getting their attention is about interest; keeping their attention is about relevance" (115).

Near the beginning of the year, with any grade I was teaching, I often had students create a page entitled Reading is Everywhere. They enjoy brainstorming all the things we read and they begin to realize the relevancy of reading.

In *Visible Learning for Literacy*, Fisher, Frey, and Hattie (2016) remind us, "Learning becomes more meaningful when learners see what they're learning as being meaningful in their own lives" (112).

When I was an assistant principal, I once had a mom come into my office in tears. When I tell this story to students, I ask them to predict why she was upset. Their first guess is typically that her child was being bullied. Other predictions include that her child struggles with reading, but no one anticipates the true reason: she herself was illiterate and came to me for help. She had kept her illiteracy a secret from everyone in her life, even her own family. Students are shocked when they realize there may be adults in their midst who are illiterate. I am always sure to reinforce that she was an intelligent woman and that you wouldn't assume her illiteracy by speaking with her. For whatever reason, she did not learn to read and write. I then ask students to think about all the things she couldn't do: read bedtime stories to her kids, read school newsletters or field trip forms, read a menu in a restaurant, read the ingredients on food packaging, write a grocery list, write an email to her child's teacher, and on and on. We talk about her inevitable coping strategies. What did she have to do to survive and function in the world? Without the ability to read and write, how might she rely on other strands of language, in particular listening and viewing? We also talk about the emotion: the shame, the sadness, the feelings of failure and embarrassment, and the feeling of fear, too. Students often ask how I helped her. I explain that I met with her a few times, but also found her a literacy tutor through a local organization. Most importantly, though, I listened without judgment.

Every class is rapt during this discussion. I share this story with students to help them understand the importance of literacy. To help them see how literacy enables each of us to fully function in the world. To spark a similar conversation, you may share and discuss this quote by Ludwig Wittgenstein: "The limits of your language are the limits of your world." After a discussion such as this, there is never again the question, "Why do we need to know this?" The answers are obvious.

The Role of Language in Learning

I encourage you to talk openly about the role of language in learning. When students think about their thinking and talk about their learning, they become more aware of their strengths and the challenges they face. "As we make thinking—our own as well as that of our students—visible, we draw attention to the mechanisms by which individuals construct their understanding" (Ritchhart, Church & Morrison 2011, 21-22). Metacognition is an opportunity for students to reflect on their own learning processes and understand what helps them learn. By applying *thinking routines* in any subject, we capitalize on the role of language in learning and provide opportunities for metacognition. Thinking routines—such as Think-Pair-Share or Connect-Extend-Challenge—are strategies that can be implemented to enhance student learning in all subject areas. We will explore some in Chapter 8: Literacy in the Content Areas, but you might also consult *Making Thinking Visible* by Ron Ritchhart, Mark Church, and Karen Morrison, as well as Project Zero from the Harvard Graduate School of Education. They provide a *Thinking Routines Toolbox* for easy reference.

Take the time to discuss these questions with students.

- When and where do we read? Why is reading important?
- What types of text do you enjoy reading? What types of text do you find more challenging to read?
- How did reading this text change who you are?
- Did your understanding of this text change after you talked with your group? Why do you think that is?
- What did you notice about your freewrite today? Did your thinking change? Do you think you would have come to this realization without freewriting?
- What helps you understand and remember what we are learning in class?
- When you are asked to represent your learning, what forms of representation do you gravitate toward? Why do you think that is?
- What goals do you have for yourself as a learner this month? What strategies are you going to use to help you learn? Think about the role of language and how you learn best.

Our classrooms are complex. As we teach literacy skills, we must use those very skills in order to help our students learn. Hattie reminds us, "When teaching and learning are visible, there is a greater likelihood of students reaching higher levels of achievement." The more transparent we are about language and how it connects to learning, the better!

3

Planning: Your Year, Your Week, Your Lessons

"The key is not to prioritize what is on your schedule, but to schedule your priorities." — Stephen Covey

To add to the complexity of planning for and teaching language arts, students use language to learn language.

For many teachers, the most challenging aspect of teaching language arts is planning. Content-based curricular subjects, such as science and social studies, are typically divided into topics or units, making planning fairly straightforward and linear. Within the language arts curriculum, on the other hand, we visit and revisit the skills and processes throughout the school year and also from year to year. In some provinces, the curriculum itself tends to be much more open-ended and therefore more daunting to many. And yet, planning is essential if we are to create meaningful, productive learning opportunities for our students.

Recognizing the Emotion Tied to Literacy Learning

Literacy learning is empowering and enlightening for many, but for others it becomes frustrating and overwhelming when they do not have easy access to the words on the page. In his book *Literacy's Democratic Roots*, Newkirk (2023) says:

> … as humans we have the great gift, the great evolutionary achievement, of speech and story. It's what we do best—and all literacy instruction needs to honor and build on that gift. It is sinful to make students feel inadequate or out of place—to silence them, to treat them as empty vessels, or to make literacy such a chore that they choose not to try. (xxvi)

Through our planning and instruction, we must find ways to recognize and build on our students' capabilities, maintaining their dignity and respect especially through challenging tasks. How—and what—we plan for literacy instruction reveals our priorities. Let's return to the words of Adam Grant (2023): "fostering a culture that allows all students to grow intellectually and thrive emotionally" (176). In my mind, the two—growing intellectually and thriving emotionally—go hand in hand, and careful planning can help us achieve these goals.

Before we look to curricular outcomes, we need to consider our students. In their article "Every Child, Every Day," Richard Allington and Rachael Gabriel (2012), outline six elements of effective reading instruction. As they emphasize, these elements don't take a lot of money or time, but they believe *every* child should have the opportunity to experience them *every* day in our classrooms as a way to build both confidence and skills.

1. Every child reads something he or she chooses.
2. Every child reads accurately.
3. Every child reads something he or she understands.
4. Every child writes about something personally meaningful.
5. Every child talks with peers about reading and writing.
6. Every child listens to a fluent adult read aloud.

As Allington and Gabriel emphasize, "Each of these elements can be implemented in any district and any school, with any curriculum or set of materials, and without additional funds." When we consider our overall planning for language arts, we must keep these practices in mind. They are easy to embed into our instructional day, and they provide experiences that all children deserve. Through these practices, students will begin to feel more confident with their literacy skills, reducing the negative emotions that some associate with literacy and learning, and increasing the positive associations for all.

The Year Ahead

Throughout this chapter, you will notice references to various processes or methods. These will be explained more fully in upcoming chapters.

You may have turned to this chapter hoping to find a complete year plan ready to print, submit to your administrator, and diligently follow and check off throughout the year. Unfortunately, there is no one-size-fits-all approach. Our curricular documents vary, our students' needs vary, as do the resources we have available. It is also necessary to be responsive to student needs and consider your context. Newkirk (2023) concurs: "Teaching is profoundly situational—and every situation is unique in some way" (xxiii). Although I cannot provide you with a complete year plan, fortunately, I can suggest ways to make planning for language arts more manageable. Even though provincial curricula vary, the six strands of language are present in all, and the research about language learning is relevant in every classroom. Therefore, the structure of our planning for language arts can be similar no matter where we teach.

Where to start? Begin by looking at the genres and text types referred to in your provincial curriculum. Some provinces have specific genres listed for particular grade levels. Some curriculum is more open-ended. Generally, there is a focus on a variety of narrative text, poetry, and nonfiction text. After looking at the specific text forms, consider the many related skills and strategies that connect to them. Although the genres and text forms are often separated in the curriculum, know that there is much overlap. The separation can help us plan and determine a focus; the actual teaching can reveal the interconnectedness.

In my first book *How Do I Get Them to Write?*, I include a sample year plan for the teaching of writing. I have taken the bones of that plan to demonstrate the connections to reading here.

Since we teach the strands of reading and writing alongside one another, plan your year with this in mind. During the school year, as guided by curriculum, students will be writing various forms of fictional narratives, poetry, and nonfiction texts. Students can and should be exposed to different forms of text all year long, but they will not be writing each of these forms on a weekly basis. If I begin teaching narrative writing in November, for example, I can plan to teach related writing and reading skills at this time. Curricular outcomes related to narratives might include story structure or plot (beginning, middle, end), dialogue, point of view, character development, setting, and so on. For efficiency of time and more effective learning, we can teach the related outcomes in both contexts—reading and writing.

There are three forms of writing that I recommend students engage in on a weekly basis: journal writing, freewriting, and reader response. You'll notice on the sample year plan that follows, these forms of writing are introduced in September and continue all year long.

The following sample plan is a potential structure you may consider when planning for the year. Look to your curricular documents for guidance about the related skills in both reading and writing. Keep in mind, depending on the specificity of your curriculum, you may not necessarily include every curricular outcome on the year plan. That certainly doesn't mean they are not being taught. For example, many of the outcomes related to oral language are addressed every day throughout the school year. When planning the year, consider what you need to do on a weekly basis, and what you might focus on at a particular time of year.

Sample Year Plan				
Month	Introduce…	Related Skills		Continue With…
		Reading	Writing	
September	• Read-alouds of various types • Freewriting • Journal writing • Reader response • Writing Groups	• Understanding various purposes of messages • Responding to texts: making connections, comparisons • Self-monitoring	• Breaking barriers • Writing as a mindset • Generating ideas and content • Revision, editing (growth mindset) • Conventions	
October	• Visual journals (earlier, if time allows) • Nonfiction text	• Understanding/interpreting various nonfiction text features	• Writing nonfiction text • Ideas and content • Sentence fluency (sentence types and forms) • Using text features	• Freewriting • Journal writing • Reader response • Writing Groups
November	• Letter writing • Narrative writing	• Understanding purposes/intent of messages • Beginning, middle, end • Character development	• Dialogue	• Freewriting • Journal writing • Reader response • Writing Groups • Visual journals

A Weekly Schedule

If you teach in a junior high setting, consider adapting the weekly schedule to fit your timetable. You will likely discover many of the same benefits as elementary teachers.

Of all the suggestions I gave as a language arts consultant, the one that teachers seemed to appreciate most was the idea of creating a weekly schedule for language arts. A weekly schedule simplifies our overall planning—a significant benefit in and of itself—but it has many other benefits too. The creation of this schedule ensures that all strands of language learning are taught and interconnected each week. We can be intentional about including various forms of writing and reading on different days. We can also embed the *gradual release of responsibility* (explained more fully later in this chapter) to ensure there are opportunities for *whole-class explicit instruction*, *guided, targeted instruction* with small groups of students, *collaborative practice* with peers, and *independent practice*. Although considering the year as a whole is important, doing so can feel overwhelming. We know the end goal, but as Newkirk (2023) suggests, "… to do something challenging, you have to focus on the immediate—the small, incremental progress you can make" (xxiv). A weekly plan makes that possible.

Keep in mind, just like the year plan, the sample weekly schedules provided here for Grades 1–2 and Grades 3–6 are just that: samples. They show how you might plan your week, taking into account the various components you want to include. Although the elements appear separate, remember that they are very much interconnected. For example, on the Grades 1–2 schedule, you will notice the inclusion of a morning message. I choose to schedule it before an explicit phonics lesson because it is an opportunity to review previous learning in this area. As discussed in Chapter 1, the morning message is an opportunity for shared reading and a way for you to ensure students are practicing recently learned **graphemes**. Although it isn't on our language arts schedule, the inclusion of calendar time with our primary students (as discussed in Chapter 1), would likely occur adjacent to the morning message.

You'll notice a reference to Talk Time at the bottom of the sample weekly schedules. Recognizing the importance of oral language in the learning process, we want to ensure our students are talking to learn on a daily basis. By including this note on your own weekly schedule, it becomes a reminder to consistently embed turn-and-talk opportunities, thinking routines, and collaborative learning strategies into your instruction.

Grades 1–2				
Monday	**Tuesday**	**Wednesday**	**Thursday**	**Friday**
Journal Writing Independent Reading	Independent Reading	Independent Reading	Independent Reading	Independent Reading
Morning Message	Morning Message	Morning Message	Morning Message	Morning Message
Phonemic Awareness/Phonics	Phonemic Awareness/Phonics	Phonemic Awareness/Phonics	Phonemic Awareness/Phonics	Phonemic Awareness/Phonics
Word Study (including introducing new word-wall words)	Small-Group Instruction/ Literacy Stations	Small-Group Instruction/ Literacy Stations	Writing • targeted mini-lesson • exploration of mentor texts • modelled/shared writing • independent writing (revision)	Small-Group Instruction/ Literacy Stations
Mini-lesson Monday • read-aloud • shared reading/ writing		Reader Response (writing in response to a read-aloud or other text in some form)		Freewriting
Talk Time will be embedded throughout the week in the form of turn-and-talk opportunities, thinking routines, and collaborative learning strategies.				

Grades 3–6				
Monday	**Tuesday**	**Wednesday**	**Thursday**	**Friday**
Journal Writing Independent Reading	Independent Reading	Independent Reading	Independent Reading	Independent Reading
Word Study (including introducing new word-wall words)	Small-Group Instruction/ Literacy Stations	Word Study (word patterns, morphology, etc.)	Writing • targeted mini-lesson • exploration of mentor texts • modelled/shared writing • independent writing (revision)	Word Study (word patterns, morphology, etc.)
Mini-lesson Monday • read-aloud • shared reading/ writing	Freewriting	Reader Response (writing in response to a read-aloud or other text in some form)		Small-Group Instruction/ Literacy Stations Freewriting
Talk Time will be embedded throughout the week in the form of turn-and-talk opportunities, thinking routines, and collaborative learning strategies.				

The Importance of Routine

With our youngest students, the Monday-morning routine is adapted slightly as I use oral language and sentence starters to scaffold my students' journal writing, especially at the beginning of the year. The tasks are the same but the approach more guided.

Another benefit of the weekly schedule is that many routines become entrenched into our practice. We know what to plan for each day and our students know what to expect. For example, you will notice that each Monday morning begins with journal writing. Students know that when they come into my classroom on Mondays, their journals (with my response to last week's entry) will be waiting for them on their desks. They eagerly read my response and begin writing. There is no need for instruction once the routine has been established. Often, I have soft, instrumental music playing in the background. After they finish writing in their journals, they place them into a bin and begin independent reading. Again, no instruction required. Over the years, many of my students articulated how much they enjoyed this Monday-morning routine. It sets a tone for the week and the consistency ensures that students know what to expect, reducing potential anxiety for some. It also provides a year-long record of students' improvement in their writing.

Some of the other routines on the schedule also help with planning. For example, when I know that I am teaching an explicit mini-lesson on Monday, I can then tie the content of that lesson into the other structures we engage in during the week. Perhaps the focus of my Monday mini-lesson is understanding text features in nonfiction text. On Tuesday that week, in the reading station, students would be asked to choose a nonfiction book for paired reading and record (or flag) some of the text features they find. All of the literacy stations, in fact, could focus on nonfiction text in some way. During my small-group instruction, I might use the nonfiction text from that week's science lessons to support students who have more difficulty reading this nonfiction text on their own. I can review the text features (the format, the intent, etc.) taught in the mini-lesson and support my readers as necessary. By following a weekly schedule, we can more easily tie other instruction and practice to the focus of that week's mini-lessons.

Independent Reading

Scheduling time for independent reading—and using that time effectively—is essential. In their article "What Reading Does for the Mind," Cunningham and Stanovich (1998) provide data to demonstrate the importance of reading volume. According to Table 3 of their article:

- A student in the thirtieth percentile reads independently for approximately 1.3 minutes per day. This adds up to about 106,000 words read per year.
- A student in the fiftieth percentile reads independently for approximately 4.6 minutes per day. This adds up to about 282,000 words read per year.
- A student in the eightieth percentile reads independently for approximately 14.2 minutes per day. This adds up to about 1,146,000 words per year.
- A student in the ninety-eighth percentile reads independently for approximately 65.0 minutes per day. This adds up to about 4,358,000 words per year. (4)

The numbers don't lie: time spent reading matters. In *The Book Whisperer*, Donalyn Miller (2009) says, "The question can no longer be 'How can we make time for independent reading?' The question must be 'How can we not?'" (51) How long should our students be reading independently each day? In *Sometimes Reading is Hard*, Robin Bright (2021) suggests,

Fifteen minutes is magic!… Carving out 15 minutes a day can make all the difference. That length of time is considered consequential in helping students improve their decoding, fluency, vocabulary, and comprehension reading skills. And it's so easy to make this a part of your daily routine. (85)

In this case, scheduling is the easy part: we can—and must—find 15 or 20 minutes for independent reading each and every day. More difficult perhaps: ensuring that students are actually reading during this time and not *fake reading*, as referred to by Kylene Beers and Robert Probst, as well as Donalyn Miller. Fake readers may think they're fooling us: holding the book open… turning pages after a reasonable amount of time… pretending to be engaged. But we know they're not actually reading. My goal as a teacher is to ensure that *all* students are reading: actually reading, and eventually, enjoying it too! I see those so-called fake readers as a challenge; I do whatever it takes to find books they will enjoy.

Book selection during independent reading is key. Dictating what our students must read during this time will only turn them off more. Instead, support them in finding a topic, genre, or author they enjoy. And, as Newkirk (2023) reminds us—in addition to choice—an independent reading program also "requires a rich set of supports: classroom libraries, time for in-class reading, book talks, modelling, and growth monitoring" (143). We *can* ensure that students are engaged in reading at this time. How? By establishing routines, surrounding students with diverse books, talking about the importance of reading, getting students excited about books through book talks, and helping *every* student find books they enjoy. It may not always be easy but it is certainly worth the time it takes.

> "If you want kids to be better readers, they must read. And if you want them to read a lot, much, perhaps most, of what they read must be what they choose to read" (Beers & Probst 2017, 124).

The Gradual Release of Responsibility

In 1983, Pearson and Gallagher introduced a pedagogical model called the *gradual release of responsibility*. This model can guide the planning of our week, and also our individual lessons. The gradual release of responsibility begins with *explicit instruction*, moves to *guided instruction*, then to *collaborative practice*, and eventually to *independent practice*. We should not teach an explicit lesson and then expect students to immediately demonstrate understanding or the proficiency of a skill. And yet, if I'm honest, I'm sure many of my lessons as a beginner teacher were exactly that. But experience and reflection can be marvellous teachers, too. After some reflection on what wasn't working, I realized that in addition to my explicit lesson, students often needed both guided instruction and repeated practice to further their understanding of the skill or content. This model—one I first learned about in my undergraduate degree—made a whole lot more sense with students sitting in front of me. If you are familiar with the work of Vygotsky and Piaget, you will recognize their influence in this model. Vygotsky introduced the idea of the Zone of Proximal Development, which speaks to what a learner can do independently and what a learner can do with adult guidance and scaffolding, and through collaboration with peers. Both psychologists acknowledged the role of language and the importance of the learner taking an active role in the learning process. The framework of the gradual release of responsibility takes all of these principles into account and can therefore guide our planning and instruction in all subject areas, not only language arts.

I Do	We Do	You Do It Together	You Do It Alone
Explicit Instruction	Guided Instruction	Collaborative Practice (without teacher guidance)	Independent Practice
teacher as **model**	teacher as **guide**	teacher as **resource**	teacher as **observer**

Gradual Release of Responsibility →

Explicit Instruction: *I do*

Explicit instruction should be embedded into our weekly schedules. In our elementary classrooms, this instruction is most effective in the form of short, intentional mini-lessons. Depending on what we are teaching, they may be as short as 10 to 20 minutes, and for older students, up to 30 or 40 minutes. Often, I include some of the other stages of the gradual release of responsibility within the mini-lesson itself.

In the sample weekly schedules earlier in this chapter, you may have noticed two opportunities for mini-lessons during our week in language arts: one on reading and one on writing. Although one of these strands takes the lead during the lesson, the two strands should still be connected. What do we teach during these explicit lessons? These are opportunities to teach specific reading strategies and writing techniques. Keep in mind that if we teach in a primary classroom, our phonics instruction will also be in the form of an explicit mini-lesson.

Guided Instruction: *We do*

To reinforce what we are teaching during the explicit lesson, it is powerful for students to begin practicing the skill—whatever the skill—with scaffolded teacher support. Shared reading and shared writing are opportunities for this scaffolded support. During shared reading, for example, your students will be reading along with you. You can be responsive in the moment and support them as necessary. During shared writing, students may suggest ideas as you scribe for them, but again, this is an opportunity to support students by modelling and thinking aloud.

In addition to the shared reading and shared writing opportunities with the whole class, you may decide that some students need more targeted support in small groups. This guided reading or guided writing instruction may take place at your classroom table while other students are working collaboratively in literacy stations.

Collaborative Practice: *You do it together*

During collaborative practice, students are working with their peers but without our direct guidance or support. For example, when students work in writing groups they have the opportunity to discuss their writing connected to the mini-lesson. The structure of writing groups facilitates feedback and collaboration which ultimately leads to revision of their writing. Although I am not present in each of their writing groups, the expectations are clear and the scaffolding is in place for students to be successful. The other effective way to facilitate collaborative practice is through the creation of intentional literacy stations. During their time in literacy stations, students—with a partner or small group—use a variety of materials to practice their literacy skills and review the concepts being taught. Literacy stations will be explained in detail later in this chapter.

Independent Practice: *You do it alone*

Ultimately, we want students to apply what they have learned to their independent work. Whether it is a reading strategy, a technique or skill in writing, or recognizing a new grapheme, we want them to transfer what they have learned into other contexts—reading and writing throughout the curriculum and beyond.

The Structure of a Mini-Lesson

Now that we have an overview of the gradual release of responsibly, let's look more closely at how to plan a mini-lesson, connecting it to the other instructional practices throughout the week.

See the recommended resources for reading instruction on page 161.

The mini-lessons used for explicit instruction should have a narrow focus. Whether the lesson targets a particular skill in reading or writing, it is important that we set a clear intention. Depending on the specificity of your provincial curriculum, you may have guidance in deciding your focus. If, for example, you teach in Ontario, you may look at section *C1. Knowledge about Texts* and decide your mini-lesson will focus on subsection *C1.6 Point of View*. The specifics for your grade level will provide an intentional target for your lesson. If your curriculum is broad, you may also look to other resources—including Chapter 6 of this book—to help determine which lessons to teach. When considering which skills to teach in writing, again, look first at your curricular document. If it includes specifics, you have a starting point. If not, refer to the writing rubric you use with students. Look to the highest level of achievement: each bullet point within the writing rubric can be the topic of a mini-lesson.

Whatever the skill I am teaching, I use these practices to guide my planning:

- Engage in interactive **read-alouds** with **mentor texts** chosen specifically for the skill/strategy being taught.
- **Think-aloud** for students to hear the strategic thinking of a skilled reader or writer.
- **Ask questions** to engage students and prompt them to talk about the concept.
- Co-create **anchor charts** for continual reference.
- Provide students with opportunities to **practice** the skill or strategy introduced.

A Sample Lesson

Let's walk through a lesson on teaching students to read and write dialogue. Before anything else, state the intention of the lesson—the what and the why:

Today we are going to learn about dialogue. Understanding dialogue can help us improve our reading and our writing. Now… What is dialogue?

Notice I have asked a question to engage students in the content. Whenever possible, leverage the inquiry process to activate prior knowledge and maintain engagement. Then confirm or clarify as needed.

You're right. Dialogue refers the words spoken by a character in a story. How can we identify or find dialogue in something we are reading?

I often create slides to guide my lessons and display visuals for students. Some slides include the questions I ask in order for students to follow along as I teach.

Yes! Dialogue can be indicated by quotation marks. I see quotation marks in this novel and in this picture book. The quotation marks go around the exact words that a character is speaking. (Provide a visual for students at this time and discuss as necessary.) Do all genres of text use quotation marks to indicate dialogue?

Depending on the grade level, or your students' background knowledge, you may want to provide a hint by holding up a graphic novel (or, for younger students, one of the Pigeon books by Mo Willems) to prompt student thinking about that particular type of text. Your next response will depend on what information your students share.

That's right. Some genres of text—like graphic novels, comics, and some picture books—use speech bubbles to indicate dialogue.

At this point in the lesson, I show students examples of various mentor text pages. To enable students to read the text, you may put the books under a document camera, or display a screenshot of a portion of the book. Initially, I am very explicit about showing students the dialogue in a text and explaining the opening and closing quotation marks. Depending on how you display the book, it can be effective to underline or highlight words that represent dialogue to make it even more visual for students. I suggest doing this with dialogue indicated by both quotation marks and speech bubbles. Also take the time to discuss what text is called if it is not dialogue. Usually, it is narration.

In my next set of instructions to students, notice the shift moving to *Guided Instruction: We do!* I show students a different excerpt of text and say,

Okay, Grade 4 readers, I want you to read me the dialogue—and only the dialogue—on the next page.

The phrase—"and only the dialogue"—is included because students will often include the *dialogue tag*, such as "Mrs. Jones explained," when asked to read dialogue. If they do, discuss this as necessary. Remind them that quotation marks go around the precise words said by a character. The character does not say, "Mrs. Jones explained."

At this point in the lesson, I ask students to look through the book on their desk (my students always have a book on or in their desks) and find a line of dialogue. Note: I intentionally avoid mentioning genres here. I want students to discover the differences between the genres themselves. For example, they will find quotation marks in most novels and some picture books, and speech bubbles in graphic novels. If they have a nonfiction text and can't find dialogue, this becomes an opportune time to discuss why.

Also notice that we're shifting the responsibility a little more, putting more responsibility onto the students, asking them to find the dialogue themselves.

> *Grade 4 readers, find a line of dialogue in the book you are reading. Hands up when you have one! Let's hear some examples.*

I ask various students to read aloud the dialogue they found. Again, I listen carefully to hear if they include the dialogue tag and gently remind them this is not part of the dialogue if they do. Although this seems like an easy task, finding a line of dialogue may be challenging for some. Ultimately, this task helps make them more attentive readers.

At this point we begin talking about the content of dialogue. With elementary students I emphasize that dialogue should reveal a character's personality: reminding them that we don't all talk the same way or say the same things. I take a book we are currently reading together (or one we have recently read) and read aloud some of the dialogue, asking students to guess who said it.

> *Listen carefully. Who do you think said this dialogue from* Harry Potter and the Philosopher's Stone? "I never thought to look in here!" she whispered excitedly. "I got this out of the library weeks ago for a bit of light reading."

As a class we can discuss clues such as the pronoun used and the content of the dialogue (*what* was said) to help determine who said it. Another example from the same book: "Oh, well—I was at Hogwarts meself but I—er—got expelled ter tell yeh the truth. In me third year. They snapped me wand in half an' everything. But Dumbledore let me stay on as gamekeeper. Great man, Dumbledore." Again, I ask students, *Who said it?* This time, in addition to content, we talk about the speech patterns as another clue.

Ultimately, we want students to understand that dialogue serves a purpose in a story, revealing something about a character and/or moving the story forward. (With older students I tend to go into more depth and detail, but this is typically enough for our young students.)

During the next part of the lesson, I capitalize on oral language as a precursor to writing. I show students a photograph and create a scenario. One photo I often use is of a waiting room at a medical clinic, showing many people of all ages. I explain that the fire alarm suddenly goes off. In the room are a grandmother, a toddler, a teenage boy, and a doctor. I ask students to say a line of dialogue that one of these people might speak in the moment. If they craft the line well— thinking about details such as content and speech patterns—we should be able to guess who said it.

During this activity, some students suggest a line of dialogue for the scenario and the class and I immediately know who said it: *"I'm sorry everyone. We're going to have to evacuate. Please stay calm."* Most students will realize this is the doctor speaking as it sounds fairly formal, compared to how the others (the grandmother, toddler, or teenager) might react. Often a student will give a line of generic dialogue so we're not entirely sure who said it. An example: *"What's going on?"* In this case, I ask the student to add to the dialogue to make it more obvious who is speaking. Perhaps they add more detail or the name of the person they're speaking to: *"Mommy, what's going on?"* By simply adding "Mommy," it becomes much more obvious who the speaker is. This scaffolded practice of (orally) creating dialogue will eventually improve students' writing.

After students have practiced creating dialogue for these four "characters," we do the same with another scenario, using a different photo with different potential characters. Students tend to love this activity, and I'm convinced they would do it all day if I let them! At this point, however, I ask students to look back on a narrative they have previously written.

> *Okay, Grade 4 writers. Look back at your story and think about your main character. How do you think your character would talk? What kinds of things would they say? Now, look through your story and underline the dialogue of your main character.*

I give this instruction knowing that some students have used dialogue correctly, some have used dialogue but without quotation marks, and some have not used any dialogue at all. After a few minutes, I say,

> *What observations did you make about your story and your use of dialogue? Turn to a partner and share what you noticed.*

Because I often ask students to reflect on their writing, they become used to sharing their observations. After they talk with their partners, I then ask some to share with the whole group. This is when I hear students reflect on their own writing: "I didn't use *any* dialogue!" "I think I have dialogue in my story but I didn't use quotation marks." "My dialogue sounds like it could be anyone talking. It doesn't sound like a teenager." "Some of my dialogue doesn't really matter to the story."

> *Okay, Grade 4 writers, here is today's challenge. If you didn't include any dialogue in your story, you are going to add one or two lines now. If you did use dialogue, first, check if you have quotation marks around the actual words your characters were speaking. I also want you think about how you could make your dialogue stronger and more meaningful to your story. Go ahead and spend some time revising now.*

As you can see, my process during this mini-lesson is very intentional, and I move through the gradual release of responsibility beginning with explicit instruction. You will also notice that both reading and writing play a role although students haven't yet written anything new. Reading took the lead in this mini-lesson.

If we think about this lesson in the context of our week, this would be our Monday lesson. On Tuesday, I would ask students to pay more attention to the dialogue in the book they are reading during independent reading—nothing more, just to notice it. Also on Tuesday, during my small-group instruction, I would work with those I noticed were struggling to identify dialogue. Essentially, this gives me the opportunity to review the mini-lesson and also to differentiate for this small group as necessary. While I am with them, the other students could be working on a variety of skills within literacy stations: some tasks might be connected directly to dialogue, but not necessarily all. On Wednesday, I would be sure to choose a book for reader response that includes dialogue so I can reinforce the technique, and maybe some of the related conventions, during my read-aloud. One of the prompts for the reader response writing might be "I noticed...." Since we have been talking about dialogue all week, students may write about the use of dialogue, but I certainly don't direct them to. On Thursday, my schedule allows for a targeted mini-lesson on writing. I would then take this opportunity to extend Monday's lesson with some further teaching about dialogue tags.

This week we've talked a lot about dialogue. Turn to a partner and explain what you remember.

After talking in partners, ask students to share with the class. This opening to our mini-lesson allows us to gather information about student understanding, and to clarify and review as necessary.

Now that you know more about dialogue, what do you think a dialogue tag is? It is sometimes called a speech tag.

After a few students share their ideas, I say,

Yes, dialogue tags tell us who is speaking, such as, "Enzo said" or "Mom exclaims." Imagine reading a novel that doesn't use dialogue tags. What would it be like reading something like that? You're right, it would be very confusing! The tags tell us who is speaking. Sometimes they are used before the dialogue, sometimes between two lines of dialogue, and sometimes at the end of the dialogue. Look at these examples.

I always share the following examples visually with students so they can see the differences as we discuss them.

Tim groaned, "I don't want to go to school."
"You know you have to," replied his mom.
"Okay, I'll go," he said, picking up his backpack, "but I'm not going to like it."

Grade 4 readers, read me the dialogue tag in the first sentence. Good. Notice that 'Tim groaned' *is at the beginning of the sentence, before the line of dialogue. The author used a comma* after *the dialogue tag and* before *the opening quotation marks.*
   Now read me the tag from the second sentence. That's right: 'replied his mom.' *Where is the tag in this sentence? Yes, this time it is at the end of the sentence,* after *the dialogue. Notice that there is a comma inside the closing quotation marks.*
   Okay, now read me the dialogue tag in the last sentence. Interesting! In this sentence, we see the simple tag 'he said,' *but we also have some description to go along with it. Does the character, Tim, say the words* 'picking up his backpack' *aloud? No. How do we know? Those words are not within the quotation marks. Where is this tag—*'he said, picking up his backpack'—*located in the sentence? Yes, it is in the middle of the two parts of the dialogue. The dialogue begins with* "'Okay, I'll go'" *and then continues after the tag with* "'but I'm not going to like it.'" *Notice that in this example, the two parts of dialogue connect directly to each other:* "'Okay, I'll go, but I'm not going to like it.'" *These two parts of sentence could have been written together, but for variety, the author chose to put the dialogue tag in the middle.*

For many classes, this is enough for a first exposure. However, I adapt the lesson depending on the group. I might go deeper if I sense the students can handle more. Other times, students are curious and ask more questions. For example, I have been asked if a comma is always used before a closing quotation mark when the dialogue tag is as the end of a sentence: *"You know you have to,"* *replied his mom.* I explain that a question mark or an exclamation mark could be used here instead, but only if the dialogue was a question or an exclamation.

With all classes, I now begin to release responsibility onto the students as I did in the Monday lesson.

Okay, Grade 4 writers, look back to this first example. Where is the dialogue tag? Right. It is at the beginning *of the sentence,* before *the dialogue. Open a book you have with you now and find a sentence that has the dialogue tag at the* beginning *of the sentence. Hands up when you find one.*

For this part of the lesson I ensure that all students have a book that includes both dialogue and dialogue tags: for this purpose, a chapter book or novel is best. Identifying the tags in different places is challenging for some students. Remember that learning to do so will make them more observant readers and, eventually, help with their writing.

After they find a dialogue tag at the beginning of a sentence, I then have them find one at the end of a sentence, and then eventually one in the middle, asking them to share with a partner or the class each time. I am sure to explain that when authors vary their sentences by putting tags in different places, the writing is more interesting to listen to, and more sophisticated even.

The anchor chart you create for this lesson could show the three possible positions of a dialogue tag in a sentence, including proper punctuation for each. Students can then refer back to this anchor chart when writing their own dialogue.

Okay, of the three places we find dialogue tags in a sentence, which did you notice the most of in your book? Which do you think is the most common placement? (The most common placement for dialogue tags tends to be at the end of a sentence.) *Which do you think is most challenging to write and format?* (Dialogue tags in the middle of a sentence.)

At this point, I ask students to return to the story they were working with earlier. This time, we turn our attention to dialogue tags.

Okay, Grade 4 writers. Look back at your story. Find the dialogue you have written. Did you also include dialogue tags? If so, notice where are they located in your sentences.

Again, I ask students to share their observations with a partner and then the class. After sharing observations, I ask them to think about what they could do to improve their own use of dialogue tags.

After this discussion, I prepare for a shared writing activity either on the interactive whiteboard or on chart paper. For shared writing, use lined pages whenever possible so you can model proper spacing and formatting.

Today, as a class, we are going to write a conversation between two characters. (Share some ideas with students and let them choose: fork and spoon, ketchup and mustard, baseball and glove, hockey bag and equipment, pet cat and pet dog, pencil and eraser, etc.) *We have to think about what these characters would be talking about, and how each of them might talk to reveal their personalities.*

When I scribe the conversation my students create between the two chosen characters, I am always sure to think-aloud: *"Okay, I'm going to start this paragraph by indenting. What do we want the first character to say?"* As I write, I'm going to talk about where to add the quotation marks and punctuation. Also, as I invite ideas from students about the content of the dialogue, I will ask where they want the dialogue tag and which verb they want to use. I model starting a new paragraph (new line and indent) each time a new character speaks. Not all students will transfer this to their own writing immediately, but some certainly do.

After we finish writing the exchange between the two characters, we read it together as a class. This is a perfect opportunity to discuss any revisions or edits we might want to make. I always make a point of changing at least one thing so students see that this is what writers do.

After the shared writing (We do!), you may choose to challenge students to begin writing their own conversation between two objects. This is an opportunity to begin practicing the skills with less scaffolding. Keep in mind, we have discussed a lot: the use of quotation marks, the placement of surrounding punctuation, the content of the dialogue, the placement of dialogue tags (sentence structure), and the verb choice within dialogue tags. I would not expect students to transfer all of these concepts or techniques into their first attempt at writing dialogue after the lesson. Learning writing techniques is a process, with students progressing at different rates.

Within these example lessons, I may spend more time on related concepts as appropriate. For example, we might explore the verbs used in dialogue tags. While we don't want students to always use the word "said", student writing will feel forced and awkward if they use a verb other than "said" in each and every dialogue tag. The word "said" can be considered an invisible word (meaning readers will not focus on how much it is used) and should not be abandoned altogether. Balance is key.

This lesson structure, working through the gradual release of responsibility, can be used when planning any mini-lesson. Become familiar with the structure but also be creative in how you approach your lessons. As Sir Ken Robinson reminds us, "Teaching is a creative profession, not a delivery system. Great teachers do [pass on information], but what great teachers also do is mentor, stimulate, provoke, engage." Following a structure ensures all elements are present for an effective lesson, but it is important to leverage your passion and creativity too.

Literacy Stations

On the weekly schedule, there are several blocks set aside for time in literacy stations. They provide the collaborative practice—the 'you do it together'—referred to in the gradual release of responsibility. It is essential that literacy stations do not become time fillers. They should be meaningful opportunities for your students to practice skills and reinforce what you have taught during recent mini-lessons.

Most often, I plan for two rounds in literacy stations with approximately 15 minutes for each round. I might sometimes adjust this timeframe depending on the group or the particular activities, but 15 minutes is an effective guideline.

Accountability

To ensure students are using this instructional time well, build in a measure of accountability. Typically, I have students complete the tasks in a scribbler or a notebook dedicated to literacy stations. (Or you might decide to have a different notebook for the stations that require them.) Bear in mind that you will certainly not have the opportunity to check your students' work each and every time they visit a station, and that's okay. However, you can check when you need to. I have found that if students only complete the activities/tasks on whiteboards, or only by using the game pieces provided, it is difficult to monitor what they are doing. However, if they are asked to record the words (or sentences) they create—even if they do it on whiteboards or with letter tiles first—we create a level of accountability. I suggest setting aside time to check their notebooks after your students' first week using literacy stations. This will give you an idea of how productive the time has been and who might need more guidance. The next time students return to literacy stations, you can discuss beforehand what you noticed in their notebooks and remind them of your expectations.

After the first week, try to set aside time every two to three weeks to flip through the students' notebooks. It's not about correcting or assessing the work since we consider the time in literacy stations as formative practice. However, looking through the notebooks might guide future instruction and provide insight into which groups are working productively and which are not.

Expectations

I often refer to my class as a *community of learners*. Individually, we all strive towards our personal best, supporting each other on our learning journeys. Building this community of learners takes time and intentional scaffolding.

When first establishing literacy stations, discuss your expectations for both behavior and academic work. Students need clear and firm expectations if they are to behave appropriately and use the time effectively. I typically begin by discussing what collaboration should *look* like and *sound* like in literacy centres. *If I were to look around the room during literacy stations, what would I see?* (Everyone engaged in a task, working with their partner or small group.) *What would I hear?* (On-task conversation; a productive, working noise level.) Also be transparent about why they will be working in literacy stations: it is time for each to practice their literacy skills, striving towards their personal best, and it is time for you to work with individuals or small groups. Their cooperation and collaboration in literacy stations ensure that you can give each group your full attention. Work towards productive independence rather than expecting it immediately.

Students must learn how to support each other during collaborative work. For example, they must be taught to give their partner an opportunity to try on their own (to read the instructions or to complete a task, for example) before jumping in to provide help. Students should be coached on how to provide support or work together when needed. When a student feels they need help, they are encouraged to ask their partner first. Modelling these interactions before going into literacy stations is a way to teach these collaborative skills while also being proactive about what we expect of them.

Instructional time is valuable. Students may need to practice transitioning in and out of literacy stations.

Students should also understand that they get into their groups and begin working immediately. The 15 minutes should not be spent finding a spot to work, setting up, or chatting about what to do at recess. Students should practice getting into their stations quickly and efficiently: in fact, in the beginning I often time my students. The goal is to take a bin, find a place to work, and set up all within thirty to forty-five seconds. At first, this seems impossible to students. But through practice they realize it is absolutely doable. The expectation is then set. If you demonstrate that you value instructional time and spend time practicing transitions, students become surprisingly quick. Also, if the tasks are engaging, they will look forward to getting started.

Within each literacy station, provide task cards for students to follow to guide that day's collaborative practice. Model the step-by-step reading of task cards for students. Although it seems an intuitive process to us, students do not always take the time to read each instruction carefully. They may not intuitively revisit the instructions as they complete the various steps of the tasks. The more explicit you are about this beforehand, the better.

When working in pairs, my students like to be "odd" and "even." Each time they partner up at a literacy station—or anytime instructions have to be read—they decide who is "odd" and who is "even" for that day. The "odd" person reads the odd-numbered instructions and the "even" person, the even-numbered instructions. Because building relationships and developing respect has always been so critical in my classrooms, students understand that we use these terms playfully and not to be derogatory in any way. In fact, I've overheard students say, "I'm feeling odd today," accompanied by giggles.

Groupings for Literacy Stations

Typically, the smaller the group, the more on-task the behavior, and therefore, the more productive the time. Most of my literacy stations are intended for pairs of students. But that doesn't mean you have to create more activities. Simplify your initial planning and creation of literacy stations by making duplicates of stations whenever possible: two (or even three) different bins (or large plastic zip bags) with the same materials inside. That way, two (or three) groups of two students can work on the same task in different areas of the classroom. The on-task behavior and the individual participation of students will likely increase compared to students working in groups of four or more.

I often determine pairs, or groups, based on ability levels or common skills students need to practice. If deliberate groups aren't necessary for the activity, I sometimes let students choose their partners. On these occasions, I remind them that their behavior and their time on task determines whether they can work with that person on another day.

Scaffolding for Success

When students go to a literacy station, they should not be doing anything they haven't done before in some way. If the activity is new to students, take the time to teach and model it to the whole class first. Ideally, have them practice the activity or routine before they are asked to do it independently in the literacy station. This gives them the opportunity to ask questions and sort out any confusion. If they have to figure something out during their time in the literacy station, two problems arise: their time is not used as effectively and, likely, you (and your small group) will be interrupted with questions. By planning ahead, you can ensure students know how to complete the tasks you put into literacy stations. If there is a new student, they can learn from the others. Ultimately, we want to build capacity so time is used well.

If students are in groups of three, they can number off: one, two, and three. Students learn to do this quickly and efficiently if it is part of your routine.

Organization of Literacy Stations

There are many ways to organize your literacy stations. In my experience, the easiest way has been to create stations within five main categories: Listening and Speaking, Reading, Writing, Viewing and Representing, and Word Study. The categories will remain the same but the activities within change. In primary classrooms, I add a sixth station: All About Letters!

I tend to store my literacy stations in bins of various sizes. Students are then directed to take a bin from the shelf (or perhaps a large zipped bag from within the bin) and find a space in the classroom to work with their partner or small group. Some literacy stations require very little prep, others a fair amount. Keep in mind that you do not have to build them all at once. Also remember that you will rotate through the stations to target particular skills at different times of the year and also to keep students engaged. Add to your collection over time.

To share which stations students will visit on a given day, you might choose to use a pocket chart to post the literacy station categories and then simply rotate the students' names or groups through the stations as appropriate. Or you might create a document you adjust each day and share on your interactive whiteboard. Just remember: smaller groups lead to more productive work, so you might have multiple groups all at the reading station.

For example, on the following chart, a class of 25 students has been divided into literacy stations for the day. The teacher is working with a small group while the others are at various stations. Notice that all the stations have more than one group of students. The students know they are not working as a group of four or six, but rather with their partner. If you have created duplicate task cards they might be working on the same thing, or you might have them choose from a variety of activities.

	Round 1			Round 2		
Teacher Time!	Jackson, Matthew, Heather			Chloe, Kai, William, Connor		
Listening and Speaking	Maria Drew	Hannah Jack		Jackson Matthew Heather	Ava Charlotte	
Reading	Sergio Ralph	Tanner Sophia		Maria Drew	Hannah Jack	
Writing	Liam Amelia	Mia Theo		Sergio Ralph	Tanner Sophia	
Viewing and Representing	Emma Lucas	Emily Raphael		Liam Amelia	Mia Theo	
Word Study	Ava Charlotte	William Connor	Chloe Kai	Emma Lucas	Emily Raphael	

Remember there is no one "correct" way to organize your literacy stations. Some teachers prefer creating more targeted stations rather than using the major categories I have referred to. For example, some have a station entitled Poetry where I tend to embed poetry within the other stations. Either is fine. Just be sure to plan ahead.

What do you include at each station? There are a myriad of options. Here are a few to get you started.

Listening and Speaking Station

I often see references to listening stations. I prefer the title of listening and speaking station. I want my students to practice both of these interrelated skills. To facilitate this, I begin with what may be thought of as a "traditional" listening station. Depending on the technology available at your school, this may take various forms: iPads, Chromebooks, or CD Players. Ideally, we want two students (at most three) to be able to listen to a text together. (Depending on the platform or technology, this may require a splitter so multiple students can listen to the same text.) To ensure they don't disrupt other groups, headphones should be available for each student.

Also consider online options such as Story Online. On this children's literacy website, well-known actors read well-known children's books. This is a wonderful resource, but be cautious of the story's timeframe as some are longer than others. You may want to include podcasts in your listening and speaking station as well. There are many podcasts developed for various age ranges and on a wide range of topics: stories, news, science, STEM, etc. Be sure to do your research to find what is available and effective. Visit the Common Sense Media website for recommendations and current favorites, or search Spotify or Apple Podcasts. Keep in mind that many students are used to viewing something as they listen. Listen to a few podcast episodes together—and discuss them—before students encounter them in the listening and speaking station. Also, at the beginning especially, choose shorter podcasts to help students become familiar with the form.

To add the speaking component to this station, create conversation cards or task cards related to the texts students are listening to. You might sometimes create conversation cards that target a specific book or podcast. However, you might consider creating conversation cards for particular genres that don't have to be connected to a particular text. Tailor them to target the needs of your students and the skill or strategy you want them to practice.

If you want to target a specific skill, you may choose the text students listen to. Whenever possible, provide students with choice in some way. For example, if they are on your digital library platform, you may ask them to choose a nonfiction book, fable, or mystery without giving them a specific title. When there is a specific text that you want them to listen to, perhaps the choice is given on the conversation card: Choose three of the following questions to discuss with your partner.

Reading Station

While the text within the listening and speaking station may be above students' independent reading level—since they are not required to decode the text on their own—as much as possible, the text in the reading station should be at a level that students can read independently. Remember, students will read books of their choice, daily, during independent reading time. Typically, I structure the reading station as paired reading, and I try to use texts that students are familiar with. This ensures they can read both *accurately* and *with understanding* (numbers 2 and 3 on Allington and Gabriel's list—page 32).

As an example, in primary classrooms, we may introduce weekly poems to help students practice using their **phonemic awareness**. During their time at the reading station, students could then reread the ever-growing collection of poems

Sample conversation cards and task cards are provided at the end of this chapter. They are quick to create but are critical to ensure that time is well spent during literacy stations. If you prefer, you may choose to create a full page of instructions for each station and put them in plastic sleeves.

with their partner. On another day, the task might be to reread the decodable books students have been exposed to over the past few weeks, or books that are within their independent reading level. Sometimes, you might provide a collection of books for students to explore all in one genre. In this case, there may be some books above their independent level, but the purpose is to expose them to various books within the same genre. Books that include a play or readers' theatre script can also be engaging choices for the reading station. After you have studied alliteration, add tongue twisters. The more you change it up for students, the more engaging the station will be.

If your class has access to a digital library, consider how to leverage its use for your reading station. On many platforms, you can assign specific books to students. You might assign a few choices based on level, a particular skill, or even the genre. Sometimes there are games and activities connected to the books that you can ask students to complete while at this station.

Once each month, I include wordless picture books in the reading station. Students *read* the book through together once by looking closely at the pictures. The second time through, they create an oral story together with their partner. For example, they might take turns telling the story page by page, ensuring their addition makes sense both with the illustrations and with what their partner said on the previous page. Don't be fooled into thinking this is an activity only for young students. All elementary-age students benefit from (and tend to enjoy) this scaffolded oral storytelling!

I want my students to spend most of the time at the reading station, reading. To maintain student engagement and to ensure comprehension, I sometimes embed something else into the time as well. I may ask students to flag text features as they read or respond to the text by recording a video on Flipgrid. I might have them do a word hunt within the text for a grapheme or morpheme they've recently learned. Just remember to ensure that most of the time at the reading station should be time spent reading.

Writing Station

Writing stations can be approached in two ways: through open-ended or targeted tasks. Most often I have a specific task connected to what we've been learning about in class, providing an opportunity for students to practice and reinforce their learning. Sometimes, however, you may want to leave the time in the writing station open-ended.

OPEN-ENDED

For an open-ended writing station, provide various materials to inspire student writing. For example, by including a variety of paper—some lined, some unlined, different sizes and materials—students have choice in what they create and how. Change the station periodically by adding items such as stickers or stamps. Consider how the things you include in the station may influence student writing. For example, by including a stapler, you might inspire book-making. By including envelopes, you might inspire letter writing. By including a variety of colored pens, you might inspire the more reluctant writers to get creative.

TARGETED TASKS

Even when the writing station connects to something specific students have learned, there is room for creativity and choice. For example, if you recently taught the purpose and the structure of letter writing during an explicit lesson,

Looking for effective wordless (or nearly wordless) picture books? Try these author/illustrators: Aaron Becker, Lizi Boyd, Matthew Cordell, Thao Lam, Barbara Lehman, Daniel Miyares, Jerry Pinkney, Bill Thomson, and David Wiesner.

the writing task that week could be to write a letter to someone of the students' choosing: a friend, a family member, the principal, a former teacher, a future teacher... the list is endless. Invite students to address the envelope and, eventually, share the letter with the recipient. By including a model of a friendly, formatted letter and envelope, detailing where the recipient and sender's name belong, students can mimic the format, reinforcing what you taught during the mini-lesson.

As another example, after teaching the lesson on dialogue, I might challenge students to write a conversation between two characters, as we did during shared writing. Again, having a sample on hand (or the anchor chart nearby) to support students with formatting and conventions for using quotation marks is essential if we want students to practice these skills. I often give this assignment to all students at the end of my mini-lesson. Perhaps the time at the writing station is time they can finish the assignment. Or it could be a second opportunity to practice writing dialogue between two different characters. Students enjoy this activity so much, it doesn't take much convincing to write another!

Viewing and Representing Station

This station is not one you often see on traditional lists of literacy stations, yet I believe it is an important one given the world today. From a young age, our students are bombarded with images and videos. Why not support them in viewing and understanding these messages?

One of the benefits of this station is the natural connection to other subject areas. When deciding on what students will view, consider other units you are teaching. In this station, students may view:

- a powerful, age-appropriate photograph of your choosing
- a collection of photographs (historical, modern, abstract)
- a collection of items (human-made or from the natural world)
- an artifact (such as an Inukshuk or an article of clothing)
- a short, animated film (CGI Short Films)
- an advertisement or commercial of some form

If you have access to a light box, you can use it to display the collection.

Although what is being viewed will change, you can create an established list of ways that students can represent their thinking. Include options such as concept maps, labelled diagrams, symbols, models, skits, posters, collages, and loose parts. If possible, include tech options as well: drawing programs or the creation of slides, for example. Each form will help students represent their learning about what they have viewed. To ensure accountability and honor students' work, ask them to take a photo of anything they create that cannot permanently stay in its original form. This is especially applicable to loose parts. As suggested with other stations, be sure students understand what is meant by each form of representation. Model each form before you add it as an option for students to use. You may also want to include examples of representations, such as a concept map or a labelled diagram, within the station for students to reference.

As I do with other literacy stations, I make sure the whole class has had an opportunity to view something together and represent their learning in some way. We also talk about how this process can support their learning in all areas of the curriculum. In science class, for example, we could ask students to create a labelled diagram to help consolidate their learning.

Loose parts are natural or human-made materials—such as feathers, twigs, rocks, bottle caps, buttons, blocks—that can be moved, manipulated, or combined in endless ways. If you are interested in learning more about how to use loose parts, look to the work of Reggio Emilia or Angela Stockman.

Word Study Station

The possibilities for word study stations are endless and provide opportunities for students to practice a variety of foundational literacy skills. Create stations to support students' development within these categories:

- Phonemic awareness/phonics (such as rhyme, **blending, segmentation**)
- Morphology (such as working with comparatives using suffixes *-er, -est*)
- Synonyms/antonyms
- Figurative language (such as similes, metaphors, hyperbole, synecdoche, onomatopoeia)
- Parts of speech
- Tier Two vocabulary
- Tier Three vocabulary

Within the preceding categories, there are many activities and approaches to take:

- **Elkonin boxes** (sometimes called sound boxes)
- Whiteboards/markers
- Whiteboards/magnetic letters
- Word hunts
- Word ladders
- Word chains
- Word sorts
- Word investigations
- Cut-up sentences
- Online resources
- Purchased games such as Bananagrams, Pop, and Spot It! Alphabet

Don't always feel obligated to use the purchased games as directed in the instructions. Often, I create a task card to fit the concept or skill I want my students to practice. (An example for Bananagrams is included on page 56.)

When creating a station using word ladders, consider using one of Tim Rasinski's resources to make planning much easier. His resources include reproducible pages for a wide range of grade levels. What is a word ladder? Put simply, it is a sequence of words that start at the bottom of a ladder. Students must work their way up the ladder by deleting a letter(s) in the first word and adding a different letter(s) to create a new word. Each rung of the ladder provides students with clues to follow so they understand how the words should change.

All About Letters!

In Kindergarten and Grade 1 classrooms in particular, it is useful to include stations that enable students to practice letter recognition and letter formation. This station tends to be the most hands-on. Consider activities such as:

- matching upper and lowercase letters
- the creation of a mini-book with the focus letter
- a picture sort according to beginning letters
- work with Elkonin boxes
- games included in your phonics program
- alphabet dominoes
- formation of letters with playdough, snap cubes, wiki sticks, or pipe cleaners

You may have many word study stations available for students to choose from on a given day, or you may direct them to work on a particular skill.

For stations that include letter formation, be sure to include laminated cards that students can trace with their finger. (These cards should include arrows to indicate how to form the letters.) In addition, think creatively about what other materials students can use to practice. You may choose to put sand, salt, or beads on a baking sheet or a cake pan—anything with a rim. After practicing tracing the letters on the cards, students can practice in the sand, salt, or beads. For a cleaner option, put the material of choice in a large resealable bag. Students lay the bag flat and practice their letter formation through the bag. If students are using wiki sticks or pipe cleaners to practice letter formation, they may need to form the shape over an outline of the letter rather than trying to create it entirely on their own.

Another student favorite is to create rainbow letters. Provide them with the outline of the focus letter(s). They start with one color and practice writing the letter inside the outline. Then, they choose another color and do the same. Students rewrite the letter many times because they are motivated to use a variety of colors.

As you can see, planning for literacy instruction can be overwhelming. Be patient with yourself as you strive to incorporate it all. Start by thinking about your year plan and your weekly schedule. Then, as you teach specific mini-lessons, return to the structure of the lesson to become familiar with how to embed the gradual release of responsibility. Eventually, it will become second nature. As for literacy stations, build your collection over time and work with a colleague whenever possible to share the load.

Sample Conversation Cards

Let's Talk Fiction!

1. **Look** at the cover and read the title of today's book.

2. **Predict** what you think this book will be about.

3. **Listen** to the story together.

4. Who is the **main character** of this story? What do you think this character was **feeling** at the beginning? What about at the **end**? Explain why you think so.

5. If *you* were the character in this book, how would you have felt? Explain.

Podcast — The 5 Ws

1. Listen to the podcast episode.

2. Discuss the topic according to the 5 Ws:

   Who…   When…

   What…   Why…

   Where…

3. What questions do you have about the topic that were not answered?

Pembroke Publishers ©2025 *Literacy Instruction Matters* by Karen Filewych ISBN 978-1-55138-371-2

Sample Task Cards

Write a Letter

1. Decide **who** to write to: a friend, a family member, or a teacher.

2. Use the format we learned in class to write your letter. Include the **date**, a **greeting**, the **body** of your letter, and a **closing**.

3. Be sure to **sign your name** after the closing!

4. Prepare the **envelope**. Where do you put the name of the person receiving the letter? Where do you put your name?

   Look at the samples to help you.

Dialogue

1. Choose **two characters**: ketchup and mustard, baseball and glove, pet cat and pet dog, pencil and eraser. (Or another two of your choice.)

2. Write a **conversation** between these two characters.

3. Use **quotation marks** and **dialogue tags**.

4. Remember to **start a new line** and **indent** each time a different character is speaking.

5. Try to give **personality** to your characters through what they say.

   Look at the samples to help you with formatting.

Pembroke Publishers ©2025 *Literacy Instruction Matters* by Karen Filewych ISBN 978-1-55138-371-2

Sample Task Cards

Bananagrams — Blends

1. Using the letter tiles, create a **blend** that we have discussed in class.

2. Create **as many words** as you can that **begin** with that blend.

3. Record these words in your scribbler.

Challenge: Can you think of any words that have this blend in the **middle** of the word? At the **end**?

Pop for Sight Words

1. **Take turns** picking a word from the Pop container. (Keep the word after your turn.)

2. **Read your word out loud** and **create a sentence** using that word.

3. On your next turn, **read your new word** and then **create a sentence** using **both** of your words.

Challenge: How many words can you collect and still create a sentence that makes sense?

Pembroke Publishers ©2025 *Literacy Instruction Matters* by Karen Filewych ISBN 978-1-55138-371-2

4

Oral Language

"Reading and writing float on a sea of talk." — James Britton

If we were to ask our students' parents which skills they want their children to learn in school, few would prioritize oral language. Since parents typically witness the rapid development of oral language skills in their children in the years prior to school, they don't see it as the priority for learning *in* school. Which skill do they tend to prioritize? *Reading.* This certainly makes sense. After all, the ability to read has significant implications, impacting our students' ability to learn in all areas of their schooling and, ultimately, their ability to function in the world. When we think about oral language, naturally, we think about the strands of listening and speaking. It might not be immediately evident—to parents or teachers—how important oral language is to the other stands of language learning. James Britton explains the connection between the strands: "Reading and writing float on a sea of talk." In fact, one might argue that oral language is the foundation of all literacy development. So although parents might not articulate oral language as a priority, as educators, we must recognize how important it is.

In 1986, Philip Gough and William Tunmer proposed their theory on reading—the **Simple View of Reading**—in the form of a simple mathematical equation.

Word Recognition × Language Comprehension = Reading Comprehension

As you can see, reading comprehension is the end goal. After all, why read if we cannot understand the words on the page? But in order to understand what it is we are reading, both *word recognition* and *language comprehension* are essential. The first part of their equation, *word recognition*, refers to **decoding** or word reading. The second part of the equation, *language comprehension* (sometimes called *listening comprehension*), refers to the ability to understand elements of language learning such as vocabulary, background knowledge, and language structures. How do children acquire these skills? Through exposure and practice with oral language.

Dr. Hollis Scarborough created what is known as **Scarborough's Reading Rope,** first published in 2001. The rope illustrates how many elements within both *word recognition* and *language comprehension* are woven together in skilled reading. Within the diagram, she breaks down language comprehension into these components: background knowledge, vocabulary, language structures, verbal reasoning, and literacy knowledge. Word recognition is broken down into phonological awareness, decoding, and sight recognition.

From Scarborough, H. S. (2001). "Connecting early language and literacy to later reading (dis)abilities: Evidence, theory, and practice." In S. Neuman & D. Dickinson (Eds.), *Handbook of Early Literacy Research* (page 98). New York, NY: Guilford Press. Reprinted with permission of Guilford Press.

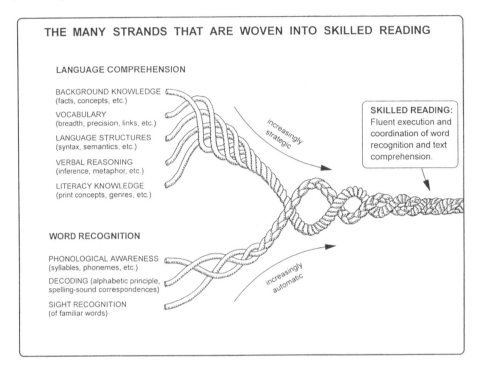

When we examine the specifics within the two main elements, the role of oral language becomes more obvious. How do children gain background knowledge, vocabulary, an understanding of language structures, verbal reasoning, and literacy knowledge if not through oral language? The rope also reveals how complex skilled reading actually is and how many factors contribute. If any one strand on the rope is missing, frayed, or broken, for any given reader, the rope is weak and reading comprehension is compromised. Student readers may need support in different areas. Therefore, the focus of instruction may have to lean or shift in different directions for different students. Understanding our students' abilities or struggles within each component will help us provide the right support to the right student.

In 2021, Duke and Cartwright proposed a model entitled the **Active View of Reading**. Building on the Simple View of Reading and Scarborough's Reading Rope, it suggests many processes that bridge the strands of word recognition and language comprehension. As you can see in the diagram, word recognition and language comprehension are not entirely separate from one another; in fact, there is much overlap when we consider connections such as fluency, vocabulary knowledge, and morphology. This model also illustrates how active self-regulation (such as motivation, engagement, and executive functioning skills) contributes to skilled reading. Some educators gravitate towards this model because it acknowledges the wide range of factors that influence reading and the role of the readers themselves.

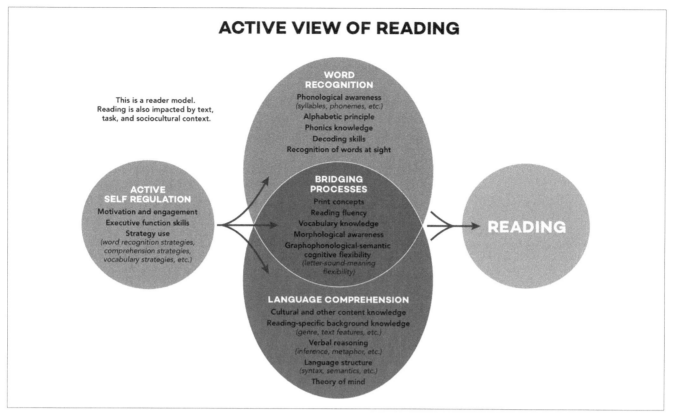

ACTIVE VIEW OF READING

This is a reader model. Reading is also impacted by text, task, and sociocultural context.

WORD RECOGNITION
Phonological awareness
(syllables, phonemes, etc.)
Alphabetic principle
Phonics knowledge
Decoding skills
Recognition of words at sight

ACTIVE SELF REGULATION
Motivation and engagement
Executive function skills
Strategy use
(word recognition strategies, comprehension strategies, vocabulary strategies, etc.)

BRIDGING PROCESSES
Print concepts
Reading fluency
Vocabulary knowledge
Morphological awareness
Graphophonological-semantic cognitive flexibility
(letter-sound-meaning flexibility)

READING

LANGUAGE COMPREHENSION
Cultural and other content knowledge
Reading-specific background knowledge
(genre, text features, etc.)
Verbal reasoning
(inference, metaphor, etc.)
Language structure
(syntax, semantics, etc.)
Theory of mind

The Active View of Reading. Reprinted from "The science of reading progresses: Communicating advances beyond the Simple View of Reading," by N. K. Duke and K. B. Cartwright, 2021, *Reading Research Quarterly*, 56(S1), S25-S44. Copyright 2021 Authors. Reprinted with permission.

Consider these examples of student readers.

Student A

Student A is an excellent decoder. If we were listening to her read, we might assume that she can understand the text because she pronounces the words correctly. And yet Student A does not have strong language comprehension skills (such as vocabulary, background knowledge, or language structures), so she cannot comprehend the text even though she appears to be reading it with ease. Even if the text were read to Student A, she would still not be able to understand the meaning because of her underdeveloped language skills.

Student B

On the other hand, let's consider Student B. This child has strong language comprehension skills but he struggles to decode or read the text on his own. He would understand the passage if it were read *to* him. But without the ability to decode, he does not have access to the words on the page and therefore cannot comprehend the text.

These examples illustrate how students may be proficient in one area but not yet considered a skilled reader by definition (or in reality) because they cannot comprehend the text. These students need support in different areas. Student A would benefit from further development of her vocabulary, background knowledge, and understanding of language structures, whereas Student B requires more support with word recognition such as phonological awareness and spelling–sound correspondences. Neither of the students have comprehension of what they are reading but the reasons—and therefore their needs—are vastly different. Burkins and Yates (2021) remind us that "children struggling with comprehension need more than comprehension strategies. They need abundant opportunities to use and develop language and to build knowledge" (21). They go on to say,

> … in the early years, while children are learning to read … we must have an eye toward the future, focusing on stretching the limits of listening comprehension through oral language development and knowledge building. (21)

When we recognize the role of oral language in relation to reading, it becomes clear why we must ensure a strong focus on oral language in our classrooms. An intentional focus on oral language will:

- build vocabulary and background knowledge
- contribute to our students' understanding of the structure and syntax of language
- improve their verbal reasoning skills
- provide opportunities to better understand content and construct meaning

"By giving our students practice in talking with others, we give them frames for thinking on their own."
— Lev Vygotsky

Oral language can be used to support learning in many ways. As discussed in previous chapters, we can capitalize on oral language strategies in our classrooms to enhance our students' understanding in all areas of the curriculum. After all, we've set up our classrooms intentionally to make for seamless opportunities to turn-and-talk. Now, after exploring the connections to reading—such as background knowledge, vocabulary, language structures, and verbal reasoning—the intentional use of oral language becomes even more important.

Once again, however, an interesting dichotomy exists in language arts. While our students are learning *through* language, we are also teaching curricular outcomes related to oral language. The outcomes—and the wording of those outcomes—will vary somewhat depending on your curriculum. The content, however, is similar:

- practicing listening and responding appropriately in various contexts
- following directions
- understanding oral language traditions
- speaking and presenting in various forms (stories, poems, reports, dramatizations)
- using and adjusting elements such as volume, tone, pace, intonation, and phrasing when speaking
- reading and understanding body language and facial expressions
- understanding how oral language assists with learning

Many of the outcomes listed here are accomplished in conjunction with other outcomes you are teaching, sometimes in language arts and sometimes in other subject areas. Capitalize on opportunities to revisit these outcomes when they arise, and don't feel constrained by the traditional timetable. If some of these outcomes are addressed during subjects other than language arts, all the better: that's integration in action.

The remainder of this chapter is divided into two sections: oral language to support learning, and opportunities to practice oral language development. Both are essential to student learning and they often overlap.

Oral Language to Support Learning

We have already discussed some ways to leverage oral language to support our students' learning. There are a few other considerations: the art of questioning, the art of listening, oral language as a scaffold, and oral language as differentiation.

The Art of Questioning

I recently saw an Edutopia post on Instagram quoting artist and educator Josef Albers: "Good teaching is more a giving of right questions than a giving of right answers." So true. Quality questions lead to quality discussion; quality discussion is thinking and learning in action. You may remember studying Bloom's Taxonomy, first created by Benjamin Bloom in 1956. Bloom's Taxonomy categorizes thinking skills, or the domains of learning, according to their complexity. A former student of Bloom, Lorin Anderson, revised the taxonomy in 2001. Anderson reversed the top two categories and changed the category names from nouns to verbs. The revisions have become widely accepted and are shown in the following diagram.

Revised version of Bloom's Taxonomy

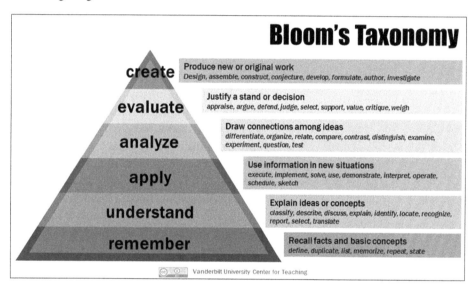

When we pose questions to students, the levels of Bloom's Taxonomy can help us target various domains of learning. For example, there may be times we want students to *remember* and *understand* ideas (considered lower-order thinking skills), but we also want to ensure they have opportunities to *apply, analyze, evaluate*, and *create* (considered higher-order thinking). You'll notice that the lowest levels—*remember* and *understand*—generally call for basic recall or explanation: one "right" answer. These may be useful when we are developing background knowledge and vocabulary. Questions at the other levels—*apply, analyze, evaluate*, and *create*—tend to be more open-ended. Students are thinking through concepts, justifying answers, making connections, and applying what they have learned. By considering the level of questioning in all areas of the curriculum, we can ensure our students have the best opportunities for meaningful conversation, ultimately leading to learning that endures.

Students, too, should learn to ask a variety of questions. Talking about the types of questions—and helping them understand the differences—can be useful. By communicating the importance of questioning—in learning, in discovery, in science—students realize the relevance and the power of questions. How do inventions and innovations come to be? Most often, through questioning—and through the exploration and investigations that occur in response to those questions. We can, and should, encourage our students to ask questions regularly throughout the day. But we can also help them develop their skills in this area through the use of images. Consider including a dedicated opportunity for questioning each week. Perhaps every Friday afternoon begins with an image of some kind (a photograph, a drawing or painting, an advertisement). Allow students to converse about the image and then generate questions—first in pairs so that all students are talking to learn, and then with the whole class. You might record some of the questions being asked and discuss the stems of those questions— who, what, where, when, why, how, could, should—and which require higher-level thinking. Even though your purpose is to help develop questioning skills, as you talk about the images students will also be exposed to new vocabulary, build background knowledge, and practice the structure and syntax of language. When choosing images, consider diverse circumstances, topics, and forms: a photograph of someone struggling through a blizzard, Van Gogh's painting *The Starry Night*, street art by Banksy, or a popular advertisement.

The Art of Listening

Although listening may seem a simple, straightforward task, I know I'm not always the best listener. Sometimes my mind drifts to something else, or I am already thinking of my response. I'm afraid to admit how many times someone has told me their name and seconds later I can't recall what it is. Listening requires attention and distractions can easily divert our attention. Most of us have to be quite intentional about listening well, our students included.

We may think of listening as passive. And it can be. Listening to music while working will likely be passive as we are not giving the music our full attention— perhaps there's no need. However, in most situations, we want our students to engage in *active listening*. Many teachers talk about what active listening looks and sounds like: eyes are looking, ears are listening, mouth is closed, body and hands are still. I understand the intent of this practice, but I am cautious about defining active listening in this way. For some students, keeping body and hands still may be challenging. A tapping toe doesn't necessarily mean a student is not listening; in fact, it might be a way the student diverts their energy to help them listen more attentively. Be open to what listening may look like for your students as individuals. On more than one occasion, I have wrongly assumed a student wasn't listening because of what I observed them doing. For some students, doodling or toe-tapping might actually help them pay attention to what is being said.

As we have discussed in other areas of language learning, ask students to think about their own ability to listen to better understand themselves as learners: *How do you listen best? What helps you to listen? What distracts you?* Just as it is important for students to understand their own tendencies, it's also important they understand the differences between themselves and their peers. Even though the expectation for most students may be that they are seated on the carpet during read-alouds, perhaps you have one student who needs to stand. Perhaps some students work best independently when they wear noise-cancelling headphones. Our discussions about listening can help normalize differences that may be necessary for students in the class.

Oral Language as Scaffolding

Oral language can be an effective scaffold in our classrooms. For example, writing is a complex skill, daunting to many students. When we ask students to write, they must generate content and communicate that content through writing. Each of those tasks are demanding in and of themselves. To support students with writing, we can capitalize on their innate ability to talk. Much of my work on freewriting with students, which was inspired by Peter Elbow (1998), is based on the premise of being able "to write without thinking about writing" just as we typically "speak without thinking about speech" (15). How we accomplish this will be discussed in Chapter 7.

There are other ways to scaffold our students' writing through oral language. By talking before writing, students can generate ideas without yet worrying about the act of writing. During a reader response experience, after the read-aloud, I ask students to talk about the text in two ways: through a reaction to the book and a connection to their own life. *"Turn to your partner and share your reaction to this book: a favorite part or maybe something you didn't like."* Once students have shared their reaction to the book, I ask them to make a connection to their own life. *"Now turn to your partner and share a connection you have to this book. What did it remind you of? What did it make you think about?"* After these discussions, I ask my students to respond to the book in writing using the prompts I provide. For example: "I liked the part when…" "I noticed…" "This book reminds me of…" Students know they can move in and out of these prompts as they wish. By talking with their partner before writing, most students figure out *what* they want to say; then, during writing, they can concentrate on the writing itself—the act of **encoding**.

In a previous chapter, I mentioned that it can be effective for our primary students to talk before writing in their journals. The opportunity to talk in this situation serves the same purpose as with the reader response writing. Let's say you provide a sentence starter for your Grade 1 students to use in their journal: "I am feeling…" Without a conversation first, many students will default to a sentence such as *I am feeling happy.* Or *I am feeling sad.* Most would know these words, and perhaps be able to spell them. By engaging students in a conversation before they begin writing, we help expand their thinking and ultimately provide more options for their writing. Discussing the variety of emotions to choose from—proud, excited, calm, disappointed, worried, scared, grumpy—as well as the possible reasons for these emotions, typically leads to more writing, and more *interesting* writing. Of course, reminding students that we do not expect perfect spelling is essential if they are to take risks and use words that stretch their phonics knowledge.

Oral Language as Differentiation

Oral language can serve as differentiation in our classrooms as well. We have mentioned the complexities of both reading and writing. Sometimes, students who are not competent with these skills are at a disadvantage when it comes to assessment in all areas of the curriculum. Think about those who are engaged and excited about your science lessons, those who can tell you everything you ever wanted to know about spiders, and yet, on a test, they are not able to demonstrate their knowledge. Was the student able to read and understand the questions? Was the student able to formulate a written answer? Unfortunately, if either reading or writing is challenging for this student, we will not get an accurate picture of this student's understanding of the content through a written test. Consider what is actually being assessed on the tests you give. If a math test is inadvertently a test of reading comprehension, we may be heading down the wrong path.

Instead, use oral language as a way to differentiate for students. If you are not testing reading comprehension, read the test questions aloud: to an individual, a small group, or even the whole class. By reading the questions aloud, a more accurate picture of their knowledge will emerge. For those who struggle to communicate what they know through writing, allow them to answer orally rather than provide written responses. Scribe for them as they talk through their answer. And remember, a science test is *not* the place to detract marks for imperfect sentence structure or spelling. Yes, we will continue to teach students these skills and set expectations for written responses, but we should not penalize students for their writing skills if we are assessing their knowledge in science.

Opportunities to Practice Oral Language

Within our language arts curriculum, there are outcomes related to communication and the exchange of ideas and perspectives. This communication, these exchanges, can occur in various forms. Build in opportunities through presentations, choral reading, debate, and by honoring the language traditions of our students.

Presentations

Being able to speak in front of one's peers is an important skill for both children and adults. And yet, it is intimidating to many. The younger we start, the better. In many instances, our students will be working in partners and small groups and sharing ideas with one another. These informal situations are important. In addition, we want students to feel comfortable presenting information or ideas to the whole class. Because we know this is stressful for many, we do not want to create a high-stakes situation for our students where they are being assessed on their presentations each and every time they talk in front of the class. Students should have many opportunities to gain confidence presenting to their peers without the worry of a looming assessment. We also want to ensure our community of learners is supportive. In time, you may choose to assess presentations on clear criteria that students are aware of. But at the beginning, each presentation should be thought of as formative practice.

A useful way to help students become comfortable speaking in front of their peers is through *book talks*. I encourage Five-Finger Book Talks. The presentation is kept simple but still provides an opportunity for students to speak in front of their peers.

Five-Finger Book Talks

1. Title
2. Author
3. Genre
4. Brief Summary
5. Recommendation

This simple structure is an easy one for students to become familiar with. You might even post a diagram of a hand showing the five elements, one on each finger. Teach students to begin by sharing the *title* and *author*. The inclusion of *genre* is intentional, meant to help students identify the types of books they are reading. Model the creation of a *brief summary* so students understand that it does not have to be long and does not give anything away. For the *recommendation*, I encourage students to complete a sentence such as: "If you like _____, you'll probably like this book." In the blank, students can insert another book title, author, topic, or even genre of text.

- *If you like Robert Munsch books, you will love this book by Jory John.*
- *If you love hockey, you will love this book!*
- *If you like novels in verse, you probably enjoy this book by Jasmine Warga.*

Through the Five-Finger Book Talks, not only do students then have the opportunity to practice speaking, but we, as a class, are exposed to new and interesting books! Typically, I schedule two or three book talks each week. Students sign up for their week so they can plan ahead.

Another way for students to practice speaking in front of the class is through the creation of presentations in other curricular areas. Perhaps students are asked to teach their peers a game that the class will try in physical education. Or perhaps you want them to present their learning on a topic in health class. Whatever the subject or topic, consider teaching students to create slides to guide their presentation. This is an excellent way to demonstrate how a main topic (title slide) is divided into various subtopics (each subsequent slide). Rather than creating slides with a large amount of information, which students tend to read from, teach them to put key points they will speak to on the slides. This process requires practice, but as you can see, it accomplishes many language arts outcomes and often those in other subject areas too.

Choral Reading

Have you ever experienced choral reading as a student? As a teacher? When used effectively, it can be a powerful way to improve reading fluency, increase the confidence of our readers, and get students talking about text. What is choral reading? Choral reading is the reading aloud of text by a whole class or a group of students. Typically, choral reading is presented to an audience. At the beginning of my career, I replaced a Grade 1 teacher on maternity leave. Much to my surprise, spring came around and I was informed that my class was to participate in choral reading at a local festival. I will admit to some nerves. This experience was not an opportunity I would have sought out myself and yet my students learned so much! Actually, so did I.

Let me be clear before you dismiss the idea: I don't see the need for a festival performance, and we can certainly engage in choral reading without an intended audience. However, there is a benefit to choral reading for an audience of some sort: the class next door, our reading buddy class, our students' parents. It might even be for a school concert. The power of that potential audience? Rereading and practice. Choral reading helps students improve both their fluency and **prosody** with a particular passage. Matching the shared voice of the teacher and their peers helps students mimic elements such as rate, phrasing, and expression. I have found that an audience—even an informal one—increases student

Readers' theatre accomplishes many of the same goals as choral reading. Students are given a script and assigned a role. The practice through repeated readings of the script leads to improved fluency. It is important to note that students do not have to memorize the scripts. As with choral reading, for best results provide an informal audience for your students.

engagement and motivation. If the choral reading is to be performed on particular date (a school concert, for example), be sure to plan ahead so students have enough time to feel confident while reading the text. Even if your presentation is more casual, I recommend setting a date as something to work towards.

Poetry is typically the text of choice for choral reading. For high student engagement, my favorites are the poems of Shel Silverstein and Dennis Lee, but any poem will work. If it is a school event, you may choose a poem connected to a particular theme. For example, the 1823 poem by Clement Clarke Moore, *'Twas the Night before Christmas*, is an excellent choice if you are preforming during the holiday season.

Once you have a poem chosen, read it to your students. Then, display the poem and ask students to read along with you, once or maybe twice. Explain that—together as a class—you will divide the poem into different parts: some lines or words will be read by everyone, some by a small group, and perhaps some by one student for emphasis. Students enjoy discussing and deciding who should read what! As they share their ideas with the class, ask them to explain or justify why they think it should be read in a particular way. Students become quite invested in this process, and are excited to work on the poem in the coming days.

Eventually, you will have a version of the poem marked up, indicating who will read what. Then, the repeated readings begin. As you practice, work towards improved fluency and expression. As students become more familiar with the text in the days following, discuss where (and how) to add more expression, and where (and how) to change the volume or pace. Once again, involve students in this decision-making, experimenting with their ideas.

The power of choral reading is not so much the end product (although it is certainly enjoyable to listen to), it is more about the process. You and your students will have opportunities to talk about the meaning of the text, the author's intent, the use of punctuation and line breaks, and much more. Without even realizing it, students will be practicing many oral language skills along the way: sharing opinions, listening and responding to each other, and making decisions about intonation, pacing, and rhythm. The discussions you have during this experience will affect how students read other text, too. As an added benefit, students who are typically nervous about reading in front of others become much more confident after the many rereadings and the support of their peers. Are you going to engage your class in choral reading every week throughout the year? Certainly not. But, occasionally, it can be an engaging and productive use of time.

Debate

Another form of oral language that tends to stir excitement in students is *debate*. Giving students the opportunity to participate in this form of exchange can help hone oral language skills—speaking and listening—while providing opportunities for critical and creative thinking. Often, the topics of debate can connect to current events, or to curricular topics in science or social studies, reinforcing the learning in those subject areas. The debates within our classrooms certainly do not have to be formal. They can occur within our classrooms when a timely topic comes up, or we can plan for a debate by choosing a topic that will fire up our students: *Should recesses be abolished? Should all students be required to wear uniforms?* Engaging in a debate is also a fantastic way to begin a unit. Take, for example, a unit about the study of life cycles or the needs of animals. You may

My two favorites for this purpose: *Sarah Cynthia Sylvia Stout Would Not Take the Garbage Out* and *Sick* by Shel Silverstein.

Many curricular outcomes are met through the process of choral reading! Best of all, it's fun.

begin the unit with a debate centered on this question: *Should zoos be banned?* Inevitably, students become invested in the topic.

I find it effective to establish guidelines before the first debate. Consider the age of your students when determining timeframes. A sample is provided below.

- **Opening Statements:** One minute per team
  Each team begins by sharing a simple opening statement explaining their position.

- **Main Arguments:** Five minutes per team
  Each team presents their main arguments.

- **Questions/Rebuttal:** Five minutes per team
  Students on the opposing team are allowed to ask questions or counter what has been said.

- **Closing Statement:** Two minutes per team

Teams present their closing arguments, summarizing and reinforcing their position.

Once you have chosen a topic, ask students to choose a side: *for* or *against.* Then, give time for students to meet in these groups accordingly. Even during this pre-debate conversation, students will be using many language skills: sharing opinions, listening to their peers, jotting notes, creating arguments, justifying their answers, and anticipating counterarguments.

For the actual debate, I suggest dividing your class into smaller groups, even if they are debating the same question. This will increase the amount of participation for each student. For example, if you have 24 students, you might run three debates. Each debate then consists of eight participants, four on each team. Depending on your goal, consider having three groups debating three different questions. That way, those not participating in the debate can vote on the topic at the end based on the arguments presented.

To encourage all team members to participate, ask the team to divide up the tasks ahead of time. Although some students shine in this structure, keep in mind there will likely be some students who are quite nervous. Group them appropriately and provide support to those who may be more reluctant.

Students of all ages can participate in debate. The earlier they begin with this form of communication, the more comfortable they will be.

Every once in a while, I had a student so skilled in debate that I would ask them to argue for the opposing side to make the task more challenging.

Honoring Language Traditions

Our classrooms are more diverse than ever before. Consider the language traditions of the many cultures represented by your students. Culture and tradition are often shared through oral storytelling, and many of our provincial curricular documents now refer to these oral language traditions.

Honor the diversity in your class by asking students to interview a parent or grandparent, an aunt or uncle, and share what they learn. Scaffold the assignment by providing support during each step along the way.

1. Develop relevant and appropriate questions to ask a family member
2. Interview a family member
3. Record the information shared by this person, perhaps through jot notes
4. Organize the gathered ideas
5. Share the ideas with their peers (provide choice in how they share their ideas)

Be cognizant of students who may not live with (or know) their biological family. Some students may be content to interview whoever it is they live with; for others this may be a sensitive topic.

Through an assignment such as this, we can build community in our class while providing yet another opportunity to practice and refine oral language skills.

The strands of speaking and listening connect to all other strands of language learning and in many ways are foundational to the other strands. Oral language strategies can be leveraged to support student learning, and the teaching of oral language skills should be an integral part of our literacy instruction. What's more, the strands of speaking and listening can be a vehicle for bringing both confidence and joy into our classrooms!

5

Word Study

"Respect the building blocks, master the fundamentals, and the potential is unlimited." — PJ Ladd

Word study provides students with the foundations for reading and writing. In order to be successful with either skill, knowledge of words and their parts is essential. When I ask a group of teachers what word study means to them, I receive a myriad of answers: spelling, spelling patterns, phonological awareness, phonics, vocabulary, meaning, connotation, context, morphology…. Word study involves so many things! Just like the strands of language must work together, so should the various components of word study if we are to provide students with the tools they need for efficient reading and writing.

Not every student who enters an upper elementary classroom has strong phonemic awareness. Teachers of all elementary grade levels should understand how to support these students.

Depending on the grade you teach, the focus of word study may lean more in one direction or another. In primary classrooms, the research emphasizes the importance of intentional, explicit instruction of both phonemic awareness and phonics. That's not to say the other areas are ignored: in fact, as you'll see in this chapter, they often build on one another. In upper elementary classrooms, the focus tends to shift from phonics to morphology so students understand conventional spelling and the meaning of many words. Teachers of all grades are going to ensure that vocabulary instruction is a regular part of their week.

In *Beginning to Read*, Marilyn Adams (1994) says:

Only if your ability to recognize and capture the meaning of the words on a page is rapid, effortless, and automatic will you have available the cognitive energy and resources upon which skillful comprehension depends. (5)

Evidently, words matter, and word study, in its many forms, is essential. This chapter provides an overview of various components of word study and strategies for effective implementation. Let's begin with the basics, which may not be as simple as we think….

Understanding the Alphabetic Principle

Letters are the building blocks for written language. The understanding that there are predictable relationships between written letters and spoken sounds is known as the **alphabetic principle**. English has 26 letters. Learning those letters should be simple, right? But did you know that those 26 letters come together to create 44 unique sounds? And as Denise Eide (2012) explains, "Those 44 sounds can be spelled in 75 different ways, 27 of which make more than one sound" (16). No wonder learning to read is so challenging!

In Chapter 1, I suggested including both an alphabet frieze on the wall and nameplates with an alphabet on student's desks. When I visit classrooms during my writing residencies, I am surprised at how many primary classrooms do not have an alphabet on student desks or tables. Often, I believe this is simply an oversight, not recognizing how complex learning to identify and form letters actually is. Even with an alphabet frieze on the wall, students also need an easy reference on their desks or tables. For some, by the time they look up to the wall to find a letter, and then turn back to their paper to print the letter, they have forgotten what it looks like. And consider the similarity between the letters b, d, p, and even q, for example. To help us understand the complexity of this learning, imagine learning a language with an alphabet other than the English alphabet. Imagine, too, that you do not have easy access to a visual reference. I know I would be both confused and frustrated! Providing students with visual tools is essential to support their learning. Recognizing and learning the visual forms of letters is only one part of this learning. They also need to understand the sounds those letters make.

As Maryanne Wolf (2007) explains:

> At its root the alphabetic principle represents the profound insight that each word in spoken language consists of a finite group of individual sounds that can be represented by a finite group of individual letters. This seemingly innocent-sounding principle was totally revolutionary when it emerged over time, for it created the capacity for every spoken word in every language to be translated into writing. (18)

Because of this "innocent-sounding principle," there is sometimes a perception that teaching these concepts to Kindergarten and Grade 1 students is easy. On the contrary, it is essential that we recognize the complexity of what we ask our young students to do: recognize and name letters, form these seemingly arbitrary shapes correctly, learn the corresponding sounds (some predictable and consistent and others not), and apply this knowledge to both their reading and their writing. Not so simple, after all!

The Reading Wars

Mark Seidenberg (2018) suggests that, "Anxiety about reading achievement underlies endless debates about how reading should be taught." (7)

There has been a long-standing debate about how to most effectively approach the teaching of reading. So much so that the term Reading Wars was coined to describe it! On one side of the debate is *phonics instruction*: teaching reading based on the alphabetic principle. On the other side of the debate is *whole language*: a method of teaching reading that emphasizes learning whole words in meaningful contexts. The pendulum has swung back and forth from one to the other, often with one area becoming a focus at the exclusion of the other.

In his book *Teaching Phonics & Word Study in the Intermediate Grades*, Wiley Blevins (2023) provides a history of phonics instruction beginning further back than most would expect: "From the time of the ancient Greeks, phonics had been taught to make written language accessible … This method of instruction continued unchallenged for over a century and a half" (24).

The debate has continued back and forth between these two main approaches, with some variation, for hundreds of years. Then, in 1990, *balanced literacy* was introduced and perceived by many to have found some middle ground—valuing both phonics instruction and whole language. At this time, levelled texts and corresponding reading assessments, such as DRA and Benchmark Assessments, were introduced. The other significant change was the introduction of a cueing system known as MSV. When students were reading unfamiliar text, they were encouraged to think about Meaning cues (pictures, background knowledge, context clues), Syntax cues (language rules and patterns), and Visual cues (using the letters and their corresponding sounds). Many teachers, including myself, were taught to rely on this system when teaching students to read. In recent years, this cueing system has become quite controversial and questioned as an effective practice, suggesting that students are prompted to guess words rather than use sound–letter associations when reading. Some school districts are even going so far as to ban the cueing system from their practice. Once again, we see the pendulum swing needlessly to an extreme. In response to the banning of the cuing system in some states, Dr. W. Dorsey Hammond (2024) published *Reading Legislation: An Alarming Development*. As he explains, "Phonics, though important, gets us only so far!" In addition to questioning the ethics of a government entity banning instructional practices, he poses this question: "Teaching students to use three cueing systems encourages them to think when they read, so are we really intent on banning children's thinking in classrooms?"

Much of the current debate around reading involves what is known as the Science of Reading (page 17). But what is it? The SoR refers to an extensive body of research, compiling data from the past few decades, on how our brains learn to read. It should be no surprise that controversy surrounds the Science of Reading too. Some question the label, and who is using the term and for what purpose. The SoR has been sold as a movement and used as a marketing tool. Blevins (2023) provides an important clarification: "It should be stated that the Science(s) of Reading is not a program and is not a philosophy. It is simply a body of evidence in how to teach children to read" (29). The data includes research from many disciplines of study including educational psychology, cognitive science, linguistics, neurology, and more. Unfortunately, this knowledge has been slow to make its way into the classroom and, until recently, many teachers have been unfamiliar with the research. Additionally, teachers have long-held, passionate beliefs about the teaching of reading. When changes in practice are suggested—or sometimes mandated—some teachers feel like their efficacy is being questioned. It is only in the past few years that the data has started to inform curricular documents and classroom reading instruction.

In his book *Reading in the Brain: The New Science of How We Read*, Stanislas Dehaene (2010) explains why the shift is occurring:

> We now know that the whole-language approach is inefficient: all children regardless of their socioeconomic backgrounds benefit from explicit and early teaching of the correspondence between letters and speech sounds. This is a well-established fact, corroborated by a great many classroom experiments. Furthermore, it is coherent with our present understanding of how the reader's brain works. (326–327)

Although I understand the passion and desire to get the teaching of reading *right,* I am always wary about the extreme swings proposed by some.

The data clearly indicates that our youngest students need an explicit, systematic focus on both phonemic awareness and phonics. It also becomes clear how these elements fit into the models of reading introduced in Chapter 4: The Simple View of Reading, Scarborough's Reading Rope, and the Active View of Reading. When situated within these models, we are reminded that phonemic awareness and phonics instruction are only a portion of effective reading instruction to be integrated into our teaching of reading as a whole.

Phonological Awareness, Phonemic Awareness, and Phonics—Oh My!

Without a course in linguistics or literacy instruction, many teachers encounter unfamiliar terminology when learning about the teaching of reading and the many components of word study. In order to understand how to approach classroom instruction, it is helpful to clarify the terminology and related concepts.

Phonological Awareness

Phonological awareness is an individual's awareness of the sound structure of words. It is an umbrella term that includes various subsets such as syllables, rhyme, **onset** and **rime**, and phonemic awareness. Keep in mind, phonological awareness is a focus on sounds and does not include print. The importance of phonological awareness is explained by David Kilpatrick (2016) in *Equipped for Reading Success*:

> The findings from countless research studies have been consistent and clear: Students with good phonological awareness are in a great position to become good readers, while students with poor phonological awareness almost always struggle in reading. (13)

Given this information, it is obvious why there is such a focus on phonological awareness in our most recent curricular documents. Providing students with a strong foundation in this area can prevent future reading difficulties.

Onset refers to the initial sound of a word (/d/ in *dog* and /tw/ in *twin*). Rime refers to the string of letters that follow (/og/ in *dog* and /in/ in *twin*).

Phonemic Awareness

Phonemic awareness is a subset of phonological awareness. It refers to the awareness that words are made up of distinct sounds (**phonemes**). Phonemes refer to the smallest unit of sound within a word. In written text, phonemes are typically indicated by forward slashes: /sh/. When saying a phoneme aloud, say the sound made by the letters: /sh/.

Is it necessary to teach phonemic awareness? Louisa Moats (2020) says,

> … one of the most robust findings of modern reading research is that proficient reading and spelling are strongly associated with the ability to identify, remember, separate, combine, and manipulate phonemes, and to do so rapidly and without effort. (26)

If we want proficient readers in our classrooms, instruction in this area is essential. The research indicates that the instruction is most effective when it is systematic and explicit, and not incidental or left to chance. If we teach Kindergarten, Grade 1, or Grade 2, we are going to embed this teaching into our daily timetable. If we teach the older grades and are working with students struggling with literacy skills, we must consider how to help students improve their phonemic awareness. As Wolf (2007) reminds us, "A child's awareness of the discrete sounds and phonemes in a word is both a critical component and an outgrowth of learning to write and learning to read" (99). The table below provides a sample script to follow when teaching the various skills involved in phonemic awareness: rhyming, isolation, blending, segmentation, deletion, substitution. Remember, this is a focus on sounds and occurs without print!

Skill	Possible Script
rhyming	*"I will say a word and you say it back to me: mad. What is a word that rhymes with mad?"*
isolation (beginning, middle, end)	*"I will say a word and you say it back to me: cat. What is the first sound you hear in the word cat?"*
blending	*"I will say the sounds. You tell me the word. /d/ /i/ /g/."*
segmentation	*"I will say a word and you say it back to me: dad. What are the sounds you hear in the word dad?"*
deletion	*"I will say a word and you say it back to me: pat. Now take away the /p/ sound in the word pat. What is left?"*
substitution (beginning, middle, end)	*"What word do we get if we change the /b/ in bat to /s/?"*

The skills in the above chart are of varying degrees of difficulty. For many students, deletion and substitution tend to be the most challenging. I recommend the Heggerty resources to support teachers with the teaching of phonemic awareness in Kindergarten to Grade 2, as they provide systematic daily lessons with an appropriate teacher script. As important as phonemic awareness is, we must recognize that these daily lessons are one aspect of literacy learning and certainly not the only focus.

Syllables

The awareness of syllables is another subset of phonological awareness. Although the previous section refers to the ability to recognize and manipulate phonemes, Moats (2020) explains,

> We do not pronounce separate phonemes when we speak. We coarticulate phonemes together in syllables, varying the articulation of each phoneme so that it blends seamlessly with its neighbours in the syllable. (60)

We do not pronounce each sound, we pronounce each syllable. Many of the words students first begin to read are one syllable: *me, can, have, think*. But most text also includes multisyllable words: *going, after, tomorrow, helpful*. Teaching students to understand syllables and connected spelling patterns ultimately helps them with word recognition. You may see references to syllable structures written in this format: CVC or CVCC, for example. Here are the most common syllable structures students will encounter:

Syllable Structure	Example Words	Syllable Structure	Example Words
V	a, I	CCVC	drum, frog
CV	me, day	CVCC	band, cans
VC	at, ice	CCVCC	drink, stamp
CVC	dog, back	CCCVC	split, street
CCV	ski, try	CCCVCC	screams, splint

An important clarification for these references: the C refers to a consonant phoneme, and the V to a vowel phoneme. They do not represent letters. A CVC word could be a word like *dog*, *pal*, or *sat*. The word *her*—even though the letters are consonant, vowel, consonant—is not actually a CVC word because it does not have three phonemes since the letters *er* say /er/. By contrast, the word *back* is a CVC word because the letters *ck* represent one phoneme: /k/.

Phonics

You've heard the word phonics, you may have even been taught through phonics … but what does phonics actually mean? Put simply, phonics is the relationship between graphemes and phonemes. Graphemes are the written representation (one letter or a combination of letters) of a phoneme (sound). In this resource and many others, graphemes are indicated with italics: *sh*. When saying a grapheme aloud, say the names of the letters: s-h.

There are three phonemes in the word cat: /k/ /a/ /t/. Incidentally, there are also three graphemes: *c*, *a*, *t*. There are also three phonemes in the word fish: /f/ /i/ /sh/. In this word, the letters *sh* come together to form one sound: /sh/. Although there are four letters, there are only three graphemes.

The letters *sh* are known as a **digraph**. In a digraph, two letters come together to create a new sound: *sh*, *wh*, *th*, *ph*, *ng*. For example, the digraph *ph* is not pronounced /p/ /h/ but rather /f/. Not all letter combinations create new sounds. The letters *bl* are known as a **blend**. In a blend, the letters retain their individual sounds: we still hear the /b/ and /l/ sounds when we pronounce this blend. English has many blends and they are often categorized according to their letters. For example, r-blends (*br*, *cr*, *dr*, *fr*, *gr*, *pr*, *tr*), l-blends (*bl*, *cl*, *fl*, *gl*, *pl*, *sl*), and s-blends (*sc*, *sk*, *sm*, *sn*, *sp*, *st*, *sw*). Some blends do not fall into these categories: *tw* and *qu*, for example. We can also teach our students **trigraphs**: three letters that come together to make a single sound, such as *air*, *igh*, *tch*, *dge*.

As referenced in the section on the Reading Wars, phonics instruction is an area where the pendulum swings the most. Many recent curricular releases have a more explicit and intentional teaching of phonics than previous iterations. Some teachers share that they never left phonics instruction behind. Others resist the teaching of phonics, perhaps not convinced of its effectiveness. Blevins (2023)

You may sometimes see the term consonant cluster instead of blend. *Consonant cluster* refers to the written form while *blend* refers to the spoken form.

reminds us that studies indicate "Early attainment of decoding skill is important because this accurately predicts later skill in reading comprehension" (17).

It's important to recognize that there is not one specific method for teaching phonics. Phonics instruction when I was a student scarcely resembles the effective phonics instruction we see today. My experience as a student revolved around worksheets: pages and pages of worksheets! Today, we understand that effective phonics instruction involves much more than isolated approaches such as the ones I experienced as a young student. Blevins (2023) suggests seven characteristics of strong phonics instruction and I have provided a short description of each. (57-58)

Seven Characteristics of Strong Phonics Instruction:
1. Readiness Skills: phonemic awareness and alphabet recognition are critical.
2. Scope and Sequence: a strong scope and sequence builds from simple to complex and provides opportunities to revisit and review previously learned graphemes.
3. Blending: the sounding out of words should be modelled and applied frequently.
4. Dictation: should be modelled regularly to help students move from decoding to encoding (also called guided spelling).
5. Word Awareness: interactive play with words and their parts, through activities such as word sorts and word building, will increase word awareness.
6. High-Frequency Words: high-frequency irregular words (those which do not follow common sound–spelling patterns) should be taught to support students when reading.
7. Reading Connected Text: opportunities to practice applying their phonics skills in text helps build mastery.

When looking at Blevins's list of characteristics, once again, you may notice the gradual release of responsibility at work. The explicit instruction and modelling (I do!), the opportunities for interactive student practice (We do! and You do it together!), and eventually independent practice within connected text (You do it alone!).

Elkonin Boxes

One strategy frequently used to help students build readiness skills and transition into phonics is the use of Elkonin boxes, named after the Russian psychologist, D.B. El'konin. This highly scaffolded approach helps students learn to segment the phonemes they hear in a word and then blend them back together. As a child listens to a spoken word, such as *cat*, they slide a counter into a box representing each phoneme, saying each sound as they do: /k/ /a/ /t/. If the word was *fish*, there would still be three phonemes: /f/ /i/ /sh/. The Elkonin box pictured here intentionally has three boxes because the words we are referring to have three phonemes.

In time, you can also have students write the graphemes that represent each sound. If they were writing the word *cat*, there would be one letter in each box because each phoneme is represented by a single letter. However, if they were writing the word *fish*, the letters *sh* would be together in one box because the digraph *sh* represents one phoneme: /sh/.

c	a	t

f	i	sh

You will also need Elkonin boxes with two, four, or five boxes to correspond with the number of phonemes in a word. At the end of this chapter, there is a page with Elkonin boxes of different lengths. Consider laminating this page for each student and providing them with a zippered bag with a few counters and an erasable marker. Then, when you teach lessons in either phonemic awareness or phonics, students have the materials on hand.

It may be daunting to teach phonics without the appropriate background knowledge. As Moats (2020) suggests, "Teachers who know more about the written code of English are more favorably inclined to teach phonics and spelling to students" (xxii). With the increased focus on phonics in curricular documents, there have been several strong resources developed to support the systematic teaching of phonics following a scope and sequence. *The Phonics Companion* by Dr. George Georgio and Dr. Kristy Dunn, and the resources from the University of Florida Literacy Institute (UFLI), are two common resources being used today. There are also many practical suggestions for all aspect of phonics instruction within the resource *This Is How We Teach Reading … And It's Working!: The What, Why, and How of Teaching Phonics in K-3 Classrooms* by Heather Willms and Giacinta Alberti.

> If you teach older students, *Teaching Phonics & Word Study in the Intermediate Grades* by Wiley Blevins is an excellent resource.

Decodable Texts

If you teach Kindergarten, or Grades 1 or 2, you will also want some decodable books in your classroom library. Levelled books—especially those at the earliest levels—include many words that are not easily decodable and can lead to frustration for our emerging readers. On the other hand, decodable books enable students to practice their phonics knowledge in context. The books follow a scope and sequence, with new graphemes and phonemes introduced gradually. They

> Do not be overly concerned if the scope and sequence for the decodable books does not match the scope and sequence of your phonics lessons exactly. They will likely be similar enough.

are designed for the explicit purpose of providing practice for emerging readers. The use of decodable books—as well as the choices available—have increased dramatically over the past few years, with the most recent releases of provincial curriculum returning to a more intentional teaching of phonics. In fact, some provinces even refer to decodable texts in their curriculum. When choosing a set of decodable books, look for text where the language is as natural as possible. As someone who has written decodable books, I know firsthand how difficult this task is for the authors with limited (and specific) graphemes available! However, the more natural the language, the better for students.

Whenever possible, project a digital version of a decodable book during your phonics instruction for students to read with you. Choose a book that targets (or at least includes) the focus grapheme. Read the text to students the first time through (many will begin to read with you), tracking as you go, and ask them to "react" each time they see the focus grapheme. For example, they may "stand up and sit back down" when they see it, or "put their hands on their head and take them off" or "touch their nose"… whatever you and the class decide. This gives you a quick visual of who is recognizing the grapheme, and also ensures students are engaged with the text. Read the book again, this time releasing more responsibility onto the students. Perhaps they can now read it without your help as you track. The multiple readings of the same decodable text will build confidence as they practice with each new grapheme introduced. In addition to these shared reading opportunities, provide students with decodable books to read independently for practice. For those who need more support, provide them with the same decodable you used with the class. For others, provide another decodable from the same set, with the same focus grapheme. Decodable books will increase our students' confidence as they practice their newfound phonics knowledge.

Sound Walls

As discussed in Chapter 1, a sound wall can be a way to display the phonemes and graphemes your students are learning. Most sound walls are divided into two main sections: vowel valley and consonants. Vowel valley will show the phoneme and the corresponding graphemes that make that sound. For example, the long i sound can be made with all of following graphemes: *i_e, i, y, igh, ie, y_e*. The consonant section is typically organized by what is called the *manner of articulation*: stops, nasals, fricatives, liquids, affricates, and glides. Many include the articulatory gestures which show what the mouth, lips, and tongue are doing to produce a particular sound.

Moving to Morphology

Morphology is the study of morphemes. A morpheme is the smallest unit of meaning within a word. Prefixes, base elements (which include bases and roots), and suffixes are all considered morphemes because they carry meaning. Consider the digraph *sh*. These two letters communicate a particular sound (/sh/) but they do not hold meaning. With the introduction of morphology, students will learn that letters also come together to create morphemes. Consider the two letters *re*. These letters form the prefix *re-* when added to the beginning of a word. This prefix means "again" or "back." For students, the realization that these letters hold meaning is often surprising since they've previously associated letter combinations only with sound. Knowing the meaning of a prefix, base element, or

Although decodable books are a fantastic way for our students to practice their phonics knowledge, these should not be the only books that students have access to and are reading in your classroom! Do not deprive students of the rich literature that surrounds them.

If you plan to use a sound wall, be sure to attend an in-service or training session to find out how they are used most effectively. Check with your school district or with other organizations offering professional development in your area.

suffix can help students better understand the meaning of the entire word. When students know that the prefix *re-* means "again" or "back," they can then better understand the meaning of words such as *rebuild, redo, reread, return, revise, rewrite,* and so on.

Three Categories of Morphemes:

1. **Prefixes:** added to the beginning of a word, for example: *dis-, pre-, un-.*
2. **Base element:** the part of the word that gives it most of its meaning. This is an umbrella term, including both *bases* and *roots.*
   - *bases,* such as *use* or *friend,* are words in and of themselves
   - *roots,* such as *-ject* or *-struct,* require a prefix or suffix to become a word
3. **Suffixes:** added to the end of a word, for example: *-able, -ive, -ly.*

For many years, when teachers asked me how to approach word study with older students, I would direct them to morphology. I recently authored a resource entitled *Bug Club Morphology* to support teachers and students in Grades 3-6. Although I thought I was well-versed in this area, my deep dive when creating the resource made me realize how much more I had to learn. I also realized how powerful this learning is for our students. As Moats (2020) confirms, "Knowing morphemes enhances reading comprehension, word recognition, vocabulary, and spelling" (134).

Have you ever seen the word *jumpt* in student work? Most teachers have! Here's the funny thing … We have been teaching our students to use their phonetic knowledge to sound out words. The students who write *jumpt* are doing just that; phonetically, this word is spelled correctly. When they understand morphemes, however, they will more likely write the word with conventional spelling, knowing that *jump* is a base and *-ed* a suffix. Among many other things, then, the teaching of morphology will assist students with conventional spelling.

In Chapter 1, I suggested including a morpheme wall in your classroom. As you teach individual morphemes you can add them to the wall under these categories: prefixes, roots, suffixes. Include the morpheme and its meaning for easy reference. (There would be no need to include bases for this context; in essence, your word wall will be full of bases!)

A Note about Pronunciation

When saying a prefix or suffix aloud, get into the habit of saying each letter of the prefix or suffix. Rather than saying "the prefix /ing/," say "the prefix i-n-g." Why? Many prefixes and suffixes have multiple pronunciations. If we say the prefix /pro/ or the suffix /ed/, for example, we are doing our students a disservice as there are multiple pronunciations of each. Students will likely assume that the prefix *pro-* is always pronounced /pro/ in a word if we refer to it as the prefix /pro/. It can actually be pronounced /prō/ as in *protest,* /prŏ/ as in *profit,* and /prə/ as in *protection.* As you can see, this seemingly simple prefix is actually quite complex.

The suffix *-ed* also has three pronunciations. If a verb ends with the letter *d* or *t,* such as *fold* or *count,* the suffix *-ed* is pronounced as another syllable: *folded, counted.* If a verb ends in a voiced sound, such as *play* or *storm,* the suffix *-ed* is pronounced as a /d/ sound: *played, stormed.* If a verb ends in an unvoiced sound, such as *press* or *dance,* the suffix *-ed* is pronounced as a /t/ sound: *pressed, danced.*

When you place your hand on your vocal chords, you can feel whether or not a phoneme or syllable is voiced or unvoiced. With a voiced sound, you will feel the vibration of the vocal chords. With an unvoiced sound, you will not feel anything because the vocal cords are not moving: the sound is made with just air.

This is why students will write *jumped* as *jumpt*. As we said earlier, phonetically this spelling is correct.

When saying roots aloud, there is no need to spell them out. Most often, they are pronounced consistently from word to word.

Prefixes

Morphemes can either be bound or free. Prefixes, suffixes, and most roots are bound morphemes. A bound morpheme requires another morpheme to become a word: *struct*, for example. Bases are free morphemes: they do not require another morpheme to become a word. A free morpheme is a word in and of itself: *friend*, for example.

Prefixes are bound morphemes placed before a base element. Common prefixes include: *dis-, in-, mis-, pre-, re-,* and *un-*. It can be effective to explore prefixes in other curricular areas too. Consider the many numeric prefixes: *uni-, mono-, bi-, du-, di-, tri-, oct-, dec-, cent-, mille-, kilo-* just to name a few. You may notice that some prefixes on this list mean the same thing. The prefixes *uni-* and *mono-* both mean "one" but their origins are different. The prefix *uni-* as in *unicorn* or *unicycle* is of Latin origin. The prefix *mono-* as in *monotone* or *monocle* is of Greek origin.

Base Elements

Most of the meaning within a word comes from the base element. Remember, a base element is an umbrella term that includes both bases and roots. The distinction between the two is important.

Bases

For consistency, when showing the different morphemes in words, underline the base element and circle prefixes and suffixes. construction

Bases are free morphemes, meaning they are words in and of themselves. They do not require another morpheme to become a word but we can certainly add other morphemes to create other words. To help students in the younger grades understand morphology, it can be effective to give them a base to begin with and ask them to add prefixes or suffixes to create other words. For example, by adding other morphemes to the base *love*, we can create words such as *loved, loving, lovely, lovable, beloved, unloved, unlovable*. By adding other morphemes to the base *rain*, we can create words such as *rained, raining, rains, rainbow, rainy, rainstorm*.

Roots

Over time, some roots have become complete words and are now used as such: *act, graph, phone,* and *scope*, as examples.

Roots are typically bound morphemes: they require another morpheme to become a word. Common roots include *dic/dict, fract, ject, rupt, scope,* and *therm*. Notice the many cross-curricular connections within these roots. It can be especially powerful to discuss the meaning of the morphemes in reference to your social studies or science vocabulary. By teaching the meaning of a root, students will gain access to many words. For example, by teaching them that *struct* means "to build" they will have a better understanding of words such as: *structure, construct, construction, deconstruct, reconstruct,* and many more. If they understand that the root *rupt* means "to burst or break" they will have a better understanding of words such as: *erupt, eruption, disrupt, interrupt, abrupt, bankrupt,* and more. Roots tend to have Latin or Greek origins. Learning the **etymology**—the origin of words and their parts—can be helpful when we are trying to determine the meaning of a word or even spell a word. Words that are connected by both meaning and spelling are considered morphologically related.

Suffixes

Suffixes are also bound morphemes requiring another morpheme to become a word. There are three types of suffixes that we tend to teach first because much of the text students encounter use them on a regular basis; students will also use them frequently as they are beginning to write. These are called *inflectional suffixes*.

Three Types of Inflectional Suffixes:

- *-s* and *-es* to create plural nouns.
- *-s*, *-ed*, and *-ing* to indicate verb tense.
- *-er* and *-est* to create comparative adjectives.

When teaching suffixes, many spelling conventions arise. For example, when you teach students to add a vowel suffix (any suffix beginning with a vowel) to a word ending in *y*, we change the *y* to an *i* before adding the suffix. By adding the suffix *-est* to happy, we create the word *happiest*.

Inflectional suffixes do not change the part of speech of a word. When adding the suffixes *-s* or *-es* to a noun (*dog, box*) to create a plural form of the word (*dogs, boxes*), the nouns remain nouns. When adding the suffixes *-s*, *-ed*, or *-ing* to a verb (*walk*) to indicate tense (*walks, walked, walking*), the verb is still a verb. When adding the suffixes *-er* or *-est* to an adjective to create a comparative adjective (*smaller, smallest*), the adjective is still an adjective.

Although these inflectional suffixes are taught first, you will also teach suffixes known as *derivational suffixes*. Derivational suffixes (such as *-able*, *-ible*, *-ity*, *-ly*, *-ness*, *-y*) are considered more complex because they usually change the part of speech of a word. The meaning of the new word is derived from the meaning of the original word. For example, take the word *love*. This base can either be a noun or a verb. By adding the suffix *-able*, we create the word *lovable* which is an adjective. The meaning of *lovable* is related to or derived from the meaning of love. Notice too, the spelling convention: remove the *e* at the end of a word when adding a vowel suffix.

Many teachers have shared how teaching morphology has influenced their students' understanding of words in significant and enduring ways.

Sight Words and High-Frequency Words: One and the Same?

As a reader, you know that not all words can be decoded or sounded out based on predictable patterns: there are some words that we just *need to know*. To support our students with word recognition, we will teach them phonics, spelling patterns, and morphology, but we also must spend time on **sight words** and high-frequency words. Although I have heard these terms used interchangeably, there are differences between the two.

Sight Words

Sight words are words that we recall instantly from memory. Some teachers believe that sight words are always irregular words—words that cannot be decoded phonetically—but actually, sight words can be phonically regular or irregular. Consider this: each of us has our own unique **sight-word vocabulary**. For example, your students will often recognize the names of their siblings by *sight*. They could be phonetically regular such as *Amber* or *Carter* but they could also be irregular such as *Siobhan* or *Beau*. (Names are often pronounced in ways connected to their place of origin.) You might also have a student who recognizes the names of dinosaurs! Are students decoding these words? Likely not. Words that students recognize are considered sight words because—by definition—they are instantly recognized by sight.

Some sight words might be high-frequency words (*the, of, said*). But not all sight words are high-frequency words. For example, your student may recognize his sister's name *Annabella* by sight, but that word would certainly not be found on any high-frequency word list.

High-Frequency Words

High-frequency words are the words most commonly used in the English language. Just like sight words, they can be phonetically regular (*in, it, and, can, went*) or irregular (*are, of, was, what, should*). Ideally—to support fluent reading—we would like high-frequency words to become part of our students' sight-word vocabulary. Believe it or not, it is widely accepted that thirteen words account for approximately 25% of the text we encounter (Johns & Wilke; Burkins & Yates). Furthermore, Burkins and Yates (2021) list 109 high-frequency words that account for more than 50% of the words that students will encounter in their reading (92).

An important note about words we consider irregular: sometimes, a word such as *have* does have an explanation behind the spelling. Although *have* doesn't follow the silent *e* rule, there is a rule that explains the spelling: English words do not end in the letter *v*. The *e* in *have* is there for a reason, just not the same reason as most words that follow the CVCe pattern. Other similar words: *give, live*.

Curious about those thirteen words? In alphabetical order: *a, and, for, he, in, is, it, of, that, the, to, was, you.*

A Shift in Instructional Methods: Orthographic Mapping

If you are unfamiliar with the process of **orthographic mapping**, you are not alone. This instructional method is new to many teachers. It is beginning to replace drill and repetition—a practice that has been used for many decades in an attempt to solidify word recognition and build a sight-word vocabulary. The practice of drill and repetition rests in the assumption that words are stored in visual memory. Kilpatrick (2016) says,

> I believe this assumption that we store words based on visual memory is a major reason why we have widespread reading difficulties in our country. *Until we properly understand how to promote permanent word storage, we will continue to have many weak readers.* (29)

We can capitalize on our understanding of morphemes to help us understand the word orthography. The Greek *orthos* means "correct" and *graph* meaning "to write." Orthography means "the correct way to write or spell words."

Fortunately, he explains, "Researchers have discovered the mental process we use to efficiently store words for instant, effortless retrieval. It is called *orthographic mapping*" (4). This process connects meaning (semantics), pronunciation (phonology), spelling (orthography), and context to lock the words into memory. With deliberate mapping, the word becomes a familiar letter string within one's orthographic memory.

Let's look at an example of orthographic mapping with the word *have*:

1. **Say the word to students and ask them to repeat it.**

   Today we're going to map the word have. *Say it with me.* Have.

2. **Connect the word to meaning and/or give context.**

   We use this word a lot. Sometimes we use it in statements like this one: I have new shoes on today. *Sometimes we use it when we are asking questions:* Have you seen Min this morning?

3. **Analyze the sounds in the word.**

   As I say the word have, *I want you to put up a finger for each sound you hear. I'll say it slowly:* have.

   How many sounds did you hear? That's right! Three.

   Try saying the word yourself and put up a finger for each sound you hear. I should hear you stretching out that word.

4. **Analyze the spelling of the word.**

   Okay, now I am going to write the word have *on the board. Look at the letters as I say each sound.*

   What did you notice? (Students can talk about the letter *e* used at the end of the word. If students are familiar with CVCe words, where the *e* at the end of a word makes the other vowel long, this is a good time to discuss that pattern and distinguish it from the word *have*.)

   You're right. There is an e *at the end of the word* have. *What sound does the letter* e *usually make? /e/. Do we hear the /e/ sound in* have? *No. Does the letter* e *at the end of* have *make the other vowel long? No, not in this word. In English, words cannot end in the letter* v. *The* e *doesn't make any sound in this word; it just prevents the word from ending with the letter* v.

5. **Connect the word's sounds with its spelling.**

   You told me there are three sounds in the word have. *Let's look at the letters that go with each sound.*

   Using an Elkonin box with three spaces, write the letters for the word *have* as you say it, stretching it out for emphasis. The last box will have *ve* together.

   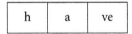

   What did you notice about the letters? That's right! The letters v *and* e *are together, making the /v/ sound.*

6. **Give students the opportunity to practice reading and spelling the word.**
   Individual whiteboards are ideal for this activity.
   Okay, you write the word with me now. Listen to the sounds as you write.
   Did you remember to put both letters v *and* e *for the /v/ sound? If not, add the* e *now.*
   Let's read it together. Drag your fingers under the letters as you read.
   Great! Now erase your board and try writing the word yourself.
   Once you're finished, read it one more time.

7. **Connect back to meaning and context.**

   A few minutes ago, I used the word have *in a statement:* I have new shoes on today. *Turn to your partner and say a statement using the word* have.
   I also used the word have *in a question:* Have you seen Min this morning? *Ask your partner a question using this word. Here's a hint: the word* have *will often be at the beginning of a question.*

8. **Connect to other words that follow a similar pattern.**

   Can you think of any other words that are spelled this way with the letters v *and* e *at the end making the /v/ sound?* (love, live)

This script can be easily adapted to map other words. Initially, use the steps and the script to help you become familiar with the process of orthographic mapping. Eventually, after mapping several words with students, you will likely feel quite comfortable with the process and no longer require the script.

Word Walls

On the day you add your word-wall words, consider orthographically mapping one of the words to help students lock the word into their long-term memory.

After the extensive focus on word study throughout this chapter, perhaps you can already see how a word wall can become a tool to reinforce our teaching. Creating the bulletin board space in our classrooms is the first step! Adding words to the word wall throughout the year is what makes this tool so powerful for students. If all of our word-wall words are posted at the beginning of the year, the word wall becomes wallpaper and few students refer to it. When we deliberately add related words each week, it becomes a living reference that students will use regularly.

With all grade levels, I playfully refer to my word wall as my No-Excuse Word Wall: *"If the word is on the word wall there is no excuse for spelling it wrong!"* This strategy works as long as we hold students accountable. For example, I ask my primary students to put up their hands when they finish writing in their journals. I circulate, listening to them read their writing out loud. As I listen, I pay particular attention for word-wall words. If a student has spelled a word-wall word incorrectly, I point it out. I differentiate this process depending on the student. If I know a student is capable of finding the word on the word wall themselves, I may simply say, *"Oh… I see a word-wall word. I want you to go find it and change it. Put your hand up when you do and I'll come check."* For students who need more support, I may underline the incorrect word very lightly in pencil and say, *"This is a word-wall word. What letter does this word start with? Right. See if you can find it on the word wall. Hand up when you've made the change."* This differentiation supports students in the ways they need. Regardless of how much support I give, I hold them accountable and demonstrate that I mean it when I say, *"Once it's on the word wall, there's no excuse for spelling it wrong!"* Not only does that one student realize that I will hold them accountable, but other students hear this as well. They are more apt to use the word wall when they know I will send them to change their work if there is an error. Even when my older students are not reading their work aloud to me, I can still hold them accountable for word-wall words. If I read something they hand in with a word-wall word spelled incorrectly, I underline the word lightly with pencil and put "ww" above it—indicating that the word is on the word wall. When they receive their writing back, I give them opportunity to fix those errors. The goal is to develop good habits and eventually to lock the spelling of these words into our students' long-term memory. If they need to refer to the word wall when writing, they do so. However, in time and with repeated practice with these words, they will be able to write these words without checking the word wall.

As you saw on my sample weekly schedules, I add words to my word wall every Monday. I typically choose three words to add at a time, and in related groups whenever possible. The first words I add are high-frequency words that I know students will be using on a regular basis. With primary students, those first three words might be *he, I,* and *she*. These are words I know students will be using regularly, and by putting them up together, I can talk about how they are related. In this case, these words are all pronouns: referring to a person without using a name. I might add more pronouns—*you, your, they, them*—the following week or in a few weeks' time. Not only are these high-frequency words, they are all on Burkins and Yates's list of 109 high-frequency words referred to earlier in the chapter (page 81).

For older students, I put some of the same words on the word wall to begin the year. For example, again I will include the word *I* but this time I might pair it with the words *said* and *because*. Why? Because they are commonly misspelled in student writing. Whenever possible, I am intentional about adding words in related groups such as *could, should, would*. These are also high-frequency words, but by adding this group of words at the same time, students tend to remember the spelling pattern especially if we orthographically map one of the words. Another effective related group: *there, their, they're*. In this case, we can have a quick mini-lesson on *homophones* (now with morphology we know this word literally means "same sound") as we put up the word-wall words. Since the word *they're* is included, you make also take the opportunity to review the idea of a contraction. Another set of homophones to add to the word wall together are *to, too, two*. By connecting the word *two* with the words *twin, twelve,* and *twenty*, students are more likely to use this spelling of *two* to indicate a number. As you can see, the words don't suddenly appear on the wall on Monday mornings, rather, this is an opportunity for intentional teaching.

Other related groups which can be effective to add to the word wall together:

- *like, make, time* (words that follow the CVCe pattern creating a long vowel sound)
- *give, have, live* (words with the CVCe pattern but without the long vowel sound; words in English cannot end in the letter *v*; see the example for orthographic mapping on p. 82)
- *what, when, where* (interrogative/question words that begin with the digraph *wh*)
- *right, write* (another set of homophones)
- *threw, through* (another sets of homophones and both words begin with *thr*)

I have had teachers ask what to do when the word wall becomes too full. Great question! First, be as proactive as possible when making your word wall knowing that there will be many words that begin with the letters *h, s, t,* and *w* and few words that begin with *q, x,* and *z*. In addition, if you find that the space for certain letters is full as the year goes on, you might take down certain words to make room for others. Invite students into the conversation about which words they are most comfortable spelling and which they would still prefer to remain on the word wall. This is a powerful conversation that encourages students to

Why is the word *I* on the word wall for all elementary students? Some students get into the habit of writing a lower case *i* for the word *I* and it is often a hard habit to break, especially as they get older. By putting it on the word wall at the beginning of the year in all elementary grade levels, we can often change their habit.

If you are removing words from your word wall, be sure students add them to their personal dictionaries first.

reflect on their own spelling abilities and again draws attention to the word wall as a tool, demonstrating the ultimate goal of locking the spelling of these words into memory.

When teachers in upper elementary ask how they can support students with phonics even when it is not a focus of the curriculum at this age, one of the most important considerations is the word wall. By building the word wall with students each week, we can be intentional about reviewing blends, digraphs, vowel combinations, etc. Students don't see this as too juvenile (as they might if we did an explicit lesson in phonics in Grade 5), but instead they see it as a way to support them with their spelling.

Vocabulary Development

Research indicates the importance of teaching all elements of language learning. As Gene Ouellette (2006) reminds us, "a teaching emphasis on phoneme awareness and phonics should not be at the expense of vocabulary enrichment" (564).

Another important aspect of word study is vocabulary development. When we use the term vocabulary, we are typically referring to our understanding of a word's meaning. When teaching content curriculum or topic-based curriculum especially, students are being exposed to many new vocabulary words. In the models of reading we looked at in Chapter 4, vocabulary was included in overall language comprehension. It really is quite staggering how many new words children learn on a daily basis. There are some estimates that they learn between six and ten new words a day. How are they learning these words? We know that it is not enough for students to hear a word once and then understand it enough to use it accurately. We must ensure they have repeated exposure to the words through read-alouds and discussion. And, the Science of Reading data also notes the importance of explicit teaching, especially in conjunction with morphology.

The Three Tiers of Vocabulary

In 2002, Beck, McKeown, and Kucan developed a model of vocabulary organized into three tiers. Understanding the three tiers helps us better support our students in learning new words.

Tier One Vocabulary

Tier One vocabulary includes words that are used most commonly in everyday conversation.

Examples of Tier One words: *chair, rain, walk, happy, clock.*

These are the basic vocabulary words that most students come to school knowing. English Language Learners or students with cognitive delays may be exceptions. Using the classroom labels that we discussed in Chapter 1 will support students with Tier One vocabulary. I would also encourage you to include a picture dictionary in your classroom library. Students learning Tier One words will gravitate to these books. There are many excellent choices but for Tier One vocabulary, I especially like those published by DK and Usborne.

Tier Two Vocabulary

Tier Two vocabulary includes what is known as academic vocabulary: words that cross disciplinary boundaries.

Examples of Tier Two words: *describe, list, explain, analyze, compare, evaluate.*

You might consider adding Tier Two academic words to your word wall as you teach them. Color-code them to help students easily identify them as Tier Two words. Or, you might want to create a separate space to post them. Either way, it's a worthwhile consideration to help bring attention to them.

These academic words are used regularly in school. Imagine your students trying to follow your instructions without an understanding of the words *compare* or *categorize*. Imagine your students trying to complete a homework assignment or test where many Tier Two words are used in the instructions. If students misunderstand the instructions, they are not likely to respond correctly and the result might not be an accurate reflection of their understanding. Teachers sometimes unintentionally neglect to teach these academic words, assuming that students already know them. Beck, McKeown, and Kucan (2013) have stated that "… instruction towards Tier Two words can be most productive" (9). We can begin teaching these words explicitly even at a young age.

When I was a language arts consultant, I often suggested that schools consider a school-wide focus for teaching Tier Two vocabulary. This is an effective way to ensure intentional teaching and reinforcement of these words for all students within the school. Remember, academic words are not specific to grade level. They are used in multiple subject areas at all grades. As a staff, you might decide on ten Tier Two words to highlight throughout the year. Every month, each teacher introduces one of the words to their class at an age-appropriate level. Perhaps the word is shared on broadcast or announcements that month, too. Create a bulletin board to help the learning become more visible. Post the academic word of the month, its meaning, and include various contexts of when the word is used. Consider the word *predict*. This is a word used in many classrooms and in many subject areas: before reading text, before an experiment in science, in social studies. I have seen teachers represent or display these contexts in creative ways. This is also a perfect opportunity to connect to morphology. The word *predict* has two morphemes: the prefix *pre-* meaning "before" and the root *dict* meaning "to say." The word *predict* literally means "to say before." By adding the suffix *-ion* which can mean "the act of," we create the word *prediction*, meaning "the act of predicting, the act of saying before." This explicit focus is sure to help students understand the meaning of the word and the various contexts it is used. Throughout the month, classes could add to the bulletin board: questions, examples of use, synonyms and antonyms, QR codes with video links… anything!

Before you begin teaching Tier Two vocabulary, you might want to explore Marzano's Six Step Process for effective vocabulary instruction.

Tier Three Vocabulary

Tier Three vocabulary refers to discipline-specific words.

Examples of Tier Three words:

equation, fraction, sum, multiply
herbivore, carnivore, species, habitat
democracy, election, parliament, community

I'm sure you were able to identify the specific area of study for each line of words. The content connections are fairly obvious with our background knowledge as teachers. And yet, many of these words would be new to students. Knowing that Tier Three words will likely be unfamiliar, many teachers provide explicit instruction. After all, understanding the vocabulary is essential if students are to understand the overall concept or content.

In Chapter 4, I discussed the idea of using images to help develop our students' questioning skills. These images can also help our students develop their vocabulary. By choosing images related to content area, we can generate discussion that will ultimately help develop our students' background knowledge, increase their vocabulary, and provide another exposure and opportunity to use these words. In Chapter 8: Literacy in the Content Areas, other specific strategies will be provided to help with the teaching of Tier Three content area words.

Spelling Tests: Yes or No?

In Chapter 7, we will discuss how spelling influences our students' writing and why a careful approach within the context of writing is essential.

We know spelling is important. If this book were riddled with spelling errors, it would detract from my message, and quite frankly, annoy many of you. Although I believe spelling is important in anything that is shared with an audience, I am not a fan of spelling tests. In my experience, traditional spelling tests do not accomplish what we set out to accomplish. Students may spell all ten words correctly on a Friday spelling test and yet, that afternoon, or on Monday, they spell the word incorrectly in their writing. Traditional spelling tests do not create transfer for most students. And isn't *transfer* the point, after all?

As you have read through this chapter, many ideas were shared to support students with spelling: a focus on phonics instruction, sound walls, word walls, spelling patterns, orthographic mapping, and morphology. By being intentional with all of these practices, our students' spelling should improve dramatically. It is often parents who want spelling tests for their children. You may have to explain how you are approaching spelling and why you are not giving traditional tests. If you do decide to give spelling tests, be sure to connect the words in a meaningful way and use one of the many strategies provided in this chapter.

Words matter. By spending intentional time studying words, you will significantly improve your students' abilities to read and write.

Elkonin Boxes

6

Reading

"Reading is a gift. And as educators, we bear the responsibility and honor of delivering that gift." — Wiley Blevins

Reading *is* a gift. We likely take it for granted if we read proficiently. I'm certainly not thinking about everything my brain is doing while I read, or thinking about everything I've learned to help me read. And yet—as we've discovered in all of the previous chapters—learning to read is complex. Wolf (2007), a cognitive neuroscientist and child development expert, explains,

> We were never born to read. Human beings invented reading only a few thousand years ago. And with this invention, we rearranged the very organization of our brain, which in turn expanded the ways we were able to think, which altered the intellectual evolution of our species. Reading is one of the single most remarkable inventions in history.... (3)

One of the single most remarkable inventions in history: high praise for this skill we expect all children to learn. But learning to read doesn't begin in school. Wolf (2007) continues,

> Learning to read begins the first time an infant is held and read a story. How often this happens, or fails to happen, in the first five years of childhood turns out to be one of the best predictors of later reading. (20)

As you can attest, some students come into our classrooms already excited about books and reading... some come to us with limited experience with books... and sadly, some come to us already frustrated. As important as it is to develop our students' reading proficiency, it is also essential to help them develop a positive reader identity. The earlier this occurs—and the more we can reinforce this attitude as children get older—the better!

When parents read to their children from a young age, they begin to understand the concepts of print—the understanding that text holds meaning, that letters form words, that print is read from top to bottom and from left to right, and how pages are turned.

Developing Reader Identity

We've discussed the many processes at work in a skilled reader, and we've also talked about the emotion tied to reading. In *The Reading Mind*, Daniel Willingham (2017) explains the virtuous cycle of reading:

> … enjoyment means that you have a better attitude toward reading; that is, you believe that reading is a pleasurable, valuable thing to do. A better attitude means you read more often, and more reading makes you even better at reading—your decoding gets still more fluent, lexical representations become richer, and your background knowledge increases. We would also predict the inverse to be true: if reading is difficult you won't enjoy it, you'll have a negative attitude toward the activity, and you'll avoid it whenever possible meaning that you'll fall still further behind your peers. (139)

I firmly believe that one of our priorities early on in the school year should be finding text to spark the love of reading in each and every student. This is especially important knowing that students who do not enjoy reading will not choose to read and therefore not get the practice they need.

This reality plays out in our classrooms daily. Students who enjoy reading excitedly dive into a book during independent reading time and are sometimes reluctant to put it down even when we've moved on to something else. We also have students in our classrooms who find reading frustrating so they procrastinate and avoid reading as much as possible. They'll take frequent bathroom breaks, have the sudden urge to clean their desks, or engage in fake reading behaviors as discussed in Chapter 3. If we're not intentional about the environment we create or the practices we put into place, the students who really need the practice reading don't get it. It is essential that we acknowledge that "Reading is both a cognitive and an emotional journey" (Miller 2009, 16). The relationships we build with our students ensure we can support them on this emotional journey of learning to read. Do our students know why we want them to be readers? Do they see how determined we are to find something that they enjoy reading?

Newkirk (2023) suggests,

> The attraction of reading is in the moment of the doing; the purpose is within the act—it is not a means to something else. We would read even if there weren't that future benefit. (144)

If you are a reader yourself, you know the joy of losing yourself within the pages of a book, of visiting another place—real or imagined—and following characters on their journey. I look forward to this escape and often think about characters I'm reading about throughout the day. Newkirk continues, "… I would argue that unless you have entered this state, the whole point, the whole gratification of extended reading, is baffling" (144). So how do we get our students to experience this joyous state?

To begin, we can shift our language to help our students think of themselves as readers. Unfortunately, many of our students don't consider themselves readers, or at least not skilled readers. I have worked with countless students over the years, in various grade levels, who say, "I don't know how to read." This perception reveals their emotional state and lack of confidence. By calling them readers, my intent is to begin to shift their concept of self.

Near the beginning of the school year, I also have my students create a heart map in their literacy notebooks entitled "I am a Reader." I was inspired by Georgia Heard's My Reader's Heart Map but I adjusted the title to help students identify themselves as readers. Before they create this heart map, we brainstorm categories that they might include: favorite books/authors, favorite places to read, feelings when I read, childhood memories surrounding reading. With these categories in mind, each student creates their own heart map. I often share mine (shown below) before they begin. The first time you ask a class to do this, consider making one for yourself to use as an example with future classes. As Georgia Heard (2016) explains, "Heart mapping gives students a chance to explore what's in their hearts and to explore how they feel, what they're passionate about, and what they deeply care about" (6).

About the same time that my students create the heart map, I also ask each of them to add a page to their literacy notebook entitled "My Reading List," where they begin a list of books they want to read. I encourage them to add to their list regularly especially after their classmates have given book talks (see page 64). Through this process, we validate students as readers. My students and I also enjoy collaborating to develop a legend to add to our pages. You could let each student create their own, if you prefer. After we read a book on our list, we return to the page to add our rating. This keeps the list active and reminds them to choose another book on their list when they're ready. If you visit the school library with your class, you may also invite students to check their list before you go, or even to bring their list with them.

Although the sample shows reading material that an upper elementary student would be reading, younger students can certainly create a reading list too.

Be an example and create your own reading list. Read books that your students are reading (and add them to your list), but also add adult titles you would like to read. Be an example even further by bringing the current book you are reading to school and read while your students are reading. A friend who teaches junior high began doing just that. She said the conversations it started about reading and reading preferences was incredible. When students see us as readers, it impacts their perceptions about reading and its purpose.

Notice that all of these strategies—calling our students *readers*, creating an "I am a Reader" heart map, and generating a reading list—promote the underlying notion that our students are readers. They're not *trying* to be readers, they *are* readers. Over time, these strategies contribute to the attitudes students have about reading. Developing their reader identity is not a one-time discussion. In fact, it should be an ever-present consideration in our teaching throughout the year.

The Power of Literature

Another way to spark the love of reading within our students is to consider the literature we share. Yes, I am going to find books that interest and appeal to all of my students for their independent reading, but I also want to share the joy of reading together through our read-alouds. Literature is a powerful tool in our classrooms. Let's face it, our world is sometimes distressing, complicated, and confusing. Our students are not immune to these realities. In her book, *Better with Books*, Melissa Hart (2019) suggests,

> Life can be difficult for both fictional characters and real kids; conflict is, after all, inevitable in this business of living. But life is also a tremendous gift, full of wonder and excitement and opportunities to make powerful connections. With this in mind, we can give young readers literature that inspires and delights, that provides

opportunities for thoughtful discussion and deliberate action, and that fosters empathy for the way they see themselves and others. (xix)

In 1990, Dr. Rudine Sims Bishop wrote an essay entitled "Mirrors, Windows, and Sliding Glass Doors." It begins:

Books are sometimes windows, offering views of worlds that may be real or imagined, familiar or strange. These windows are also sliding glass doors, and readers have only to walk through in imagination to become part of whatever world has been created or recreated by the author.

Reading—as both Hart and Dr. Bishop describe the experience—is enticing: an opportunity, even. We can experience things both positive and negative through the words on the page. Thankfully, most of our students do not experience homelessness, but books such as *Fly Away Home* by Eve Bunting, *Crenshaw* by Katherine Applegate, or *No Fixed Address* by Susan Nielsen provide a window into the reality for some families. By putting themselves in the position of the characters, the books may become sliding glass doors.

Bishop also stresses how important it is for students to see themselves reflected in the books they read: to "see our own lives and experiences as part of the larger human experience." When choosing books to read to our classes, it is important that we are deliberate in choosing characters and authors of diverse backgrounds so one voice or one perspective does not dominate the broader narrative unfolding in our classrooms.

Dr. Bishop explains:

When children cannot find themselves reflected in the books they read, or when the images they see are distorted, negative, or laughable, they learn a powerful lesson about how they are devalued in the society of which they are a part.

This is an important consideration and one that teachers have told me that they haven't always thought about. Thankfully, the publishing world has become more cognizant of amplifying diverse voices and representing a variety of experiences. Some might think that diverse books are only important for the groups being represented, but Dr. Bishop explains how this literature is essential for everyone:

Children from dominant social groups have always found their mirrors in books, but they, too, have suffered from the lack of availability of books about others. They need the books as windows onto reality, not just on imaginary worlds. They need books that will help them understand the multicultural nature of the world they live in, and their place as a member of just one group, as well as their connections to all other humans.

Although Dr. Bishop wrote this over three decades ago, it seems even more relevant today. Our students may be developing their reader identities in our classrooms, but they are, in fact, developing their identities in a broader sense too. Ultimately, through the books they read, they are learning about themselves and their place in the world. In her book *Unselfie: Why Empathetic Kids Succeed in Our All-About-Me World*, Michele Borba (2016) cites research that indicates, "people who read fiction are more capable of understanding others, empathizing and seeing another person's point of view than those who read nonfiction"

Know your class. If there is a student (or parent or sibling) experiencing homelessness—or any other topic that might evoke painful emotions—think carefully about choosing books on this topic.

(78–79). I have experienced this myself. There are books I have read that have not only stayed with me, but have changed me. Books which provided experiences other than ones I have known in my own life: memoirs such as *A House in the Sky* by Amanda Lindhout and *From the Ashes* by Jesse Thistle, and fiction such as *All My Puny Sorrows* by Miriam Toews, *The Nightingale* by Kristin Hannah, and *The Invention of Wings* by Sue Monk Kidd. Reading books like these gives me a greater appreciation of my own circumstances and helps me better understand and empathize with others. The books we choose in our classrooms serve the same purpose, whether we recognize it or not.

In 2009, author Chimamanda Ngozi Adichie gave a TED Talk entitled "The Danger of a Single Story." She emphasizes how a single story has the potential to create stereotypes and sometimes rob individuals of their dignity. By sharing multiple stories or angles on the same topic, we provide our students with a more accurate narrative. Often, when I read a book about a particular topic to my students, I will later share other books on the same topic. Perhaps my students and I have read one story about refugees or immigration. I will then share other books—if possible, in other genres—to layer the narrative and provide other perspectives about this topic. The picture books *Islandborn* by Junot Diaz, *Out* by Angela May George, and *Stepping Stones* by Margriet Ruurs are a few favorites. Depending on the age of my students, I might also share novels such as *Refugee* by Alan Gratz; *The Cricket War* by Tho Pham and Sandra McTavish; *Inside Out and Back Again*, a novel in verse by Thanhha Lai; and *When Stars are Scattered*, a graphic novel by Victoria Jamieson and Omar Mohamed. I recently read *Patty Dreams* by Nadia L. Hohn and was thinking what a wonderful addition this would be to the conversation about immigration. Although the focus of the book isn't immigration itself, the move from one country to another plays an important role in this story of transformation.

When choosing books to read aloud, share literature that is both classic and current. Be wary of reading book after book with a similar narrator. (After making this point in a session I was leading, a teacher once shared that she realized that all her novel-length read-alouds that year had a female protagonist.) Find diverse protagonists in diverse situations.

As powerful as narrative texts can be, expose your students to books from all genres: fiction (picture books, beginning chapter books, graphic novels, novels, plays), nonfiction (informational texts, biographies, cookbooks, manuals), magazines, poetry, and digital text. In fact, in most provincial curricula, there are references to the genres and types of text that should be used in elementary classrooms; there are often outcomes targeting text forms, text patterns, and text features. Refer to your curricular document for specifics. And remember, even when teaching these outcomes, the books we choose convey a message to our students—subconsciously or not.

Fluency

The most updated provincial curricular documents include an explicit focus on fluency.

Have you ever heard a student reading word by word, sounding out each word as they go? Almost in a robotic voice? It's tough to listen to. And we know that they will have little or no comprehension of what they're reading by the time they get to the end of the sentence because they are concentrating so hard on decoding each word. In contrast to the choppiness of word by word reading, a fluent reader reads with flow, automaticity, and prosody. Prosody refers to the ability to read with expression, including elements such as phrasing, pitch, rhythm, intonation, tone, and emphasis. Someone reading with prosody evidently understands what they are reading: they couldn't add appropriate emphasis or expression if they didn't.

Think about someone you know who is a strong reader—child or adult. What do you notice about their reading? Likely, you're thinking about someone who reads expressively, pauses appropriately to create phrasing, and conveys meaning through the words they read. Kilpatrick (2016) explains,

> For good readers, word reading is fluent. Fluent means fast and accurate, and includes proper expression. Fluent readers comprehend more of what they read because they can focus their attention on the meaning, not on figuring out the words. (3)

Fluency is often considered the bridge between word recognition and comprehension. And yet, many teachers have shared that they don't quite know how to teach fluency to their students. To begin, remember that all of your work on word recognition in its various forms—phonics, morphology, sight words, high-frequency words, and orthographic mapping—will support students in reading with more automaticity, leading to greater fluency.

In addition to the various components of word study, there are other strategies to support students in improving their fluency. Perhaps the most important is reading aloud to your students: it is essential they hear skilled reading. Rather than rushing through your read-alouds, take the time to add appropriate expression, phrasing, and intonation. You likely do much of this naturally but pay a little more attention to the quality of your reading, remembering that you are a model for students. Sometimes I purposely read robotically or quickly without attention to punctuation to make obvious the contrast to fluent reading. In these situations, students recognize that "It doesn't sound good" or "It's hard to understand" or even "It sounds boring." You may ask students to read a passage to themselves in this way too. They'll enjoy the task but it will also help them pay more attention to flow and prosody when trying to read fluently.

Although modelling is essential, there are also explicit mini-lessons that you can teach in regard to fluency. For example, teach the specific functions of punctuation (commas, periods, question marks, exclamation marks, and quotation marks) and how they relate to effective phrasing. Teach the features of prosody (loud and soft stresses, expression, intonation, pausing) and how they relate to comprehension. After each of these lessons, provide time for students to practice reading with the recent lesson in mind: during literacy stations or paired reading, for example. Even when they read out loud, students don't always realize how they sound. Create opportunities for students to hear themselves reading. How might they record themselves reading and listen back? Consider the technology you have available. Some digital libraries have a feature such as this within the platform. When students hear themselves, they are often surprised how quickly (or slowly) they read, how little expression they use, and sometimes they realize that they don't stop at punctuation marks. There is no need for you or anyone else to hear these recordings: they are meant as opportunities for students to practice and refine their reading. After this experience, be sure to ask students to reflect on and make observations about their fluency.

Choral reading and readers' theatre (as discussed in Chapter 4) are wonderful opportunities for shared reading and mini-lessons connected to fluency. Students—with your support—will decide on appropriate phrasing, pacing,

If your students are asked to read aloud in front of their peers or other audience—on announcements, at an assembly or concert—give them ample time to practice reading the chosen text. If they read it for the first time in the moment, they will not be as fluent as they could be with practice. Empower students and prevent embarrassment.

Although this chapter focuses on developing our students' oral reading fluency, explain to students that fluency is important when they are reading silently too, helping them comprehend what they are reading. Encourage students to practice reading fluently during independent reading.

expression, intonation, and emphasis. Both choral reading and readers' theatre motivate students to reread text which we know is essential in gaining fluency.

Comprehension

Regardless of the intent of the text—to entertain, inform, or instruct—ultimately, the end goal of reading is comprehension. After all, why read if we cannot comprehend what we are reading?

Think back to Scarborough's Reading Rope (see page 58). If a student does not understand what they are reading, in order to help them, we must determine what aspect of reading—which of the smaller strands of the rope—is causing the difficulty.

Willingham (2017) provides this example:

> … when a beginning reader uses the letter–sound translation process (i.e., sounds a word out), her working memory is occupied mostly by translation rules—"let's see, 'o' usually sounds like **aw**, but when there are two of them, 'oo,' they make a different sound…. what was it again?" That leaves little working memory space for the task of comprehension, for actually understanding the meaning of what she's read. (65)

Likely, this student is not comprehending what she is reading. What kind of support would you provide if she were in your class? A focus on word recognition, specifically phonemic awareness and orthographic mapping, would be a good place to begin. This example serves as a reminder that students who struggle with comprehension do not always need immediate work on comprehension strategies. For this reader, the support required is at a foundational level.

Willingham (2017) reminds us of the complexity of reading comprehension itself:

> … reading comprehension seems to be composed of three processes. The reader (1) extracts ideas from sentences, (2) connects these ideas to one another, and (3) builds some more general idea of what the text is about. (107)

These three processes can guide us when we are teaching students to understand text. In fact, our think-alouds should model these three processes during a read-aloud.

Fountas and Pinnell created a graphic called the Systems of Strategic Actions, which can be found on the inside front cover of *The Literacy Continuum* (2016). This graphic shows the complex thinking required of readers to meaningfully engage in text. It is divided into three ways of thinking which, to some extent, echo the processes indicated by Willingham above.

1. Thinking Within the Text
   - Searching for and Using Information
   - Monitoring and Self-Correcting
   - Solving Words
   - Maintaining Fluency
   - Adjusting
   - Summarizing

2. Thinking Beyond the Text
   - Predicting
   - Making Connections
   - Synthesizing
   - Inferring
3. Thinking About the Text
   - Analyzing
   - Critiquing

As you teach various strategies—such as predicting or inferring—consider co-constructing an anchor chart to post in the classroom. You might also have students create their own version in their literacy notebooks. (Connect to morphology when you can!)

The first section—Thinking Within the Text—focuses on word recognition and understanding the literal meaning of a text. If our students are concentrating on word recognition, they will have limited comprehension of what they are reading—as in Willingham's example above. The second section—Thinking Beyond the Text—helps students acquire a deeper understanding of what they've read by making connections to their own experiences, their background knowledge, and their understanding of the world. A skilled reader will take these connections and revise their understanding based on what they've read. The third section—Thinking About the Text—is where we as readers take the author's intentions into account. We consider the craft moves of the writer such as text type, purpose of the text, and a host of creative decisions. These three categories can guide us when devising lessons in comprehension. In fact, you will notice much of the same language used in your curriculum when referring to comprehension strategies.

Moving beyond a literal understanding of text is essential to comprehension. Consider the nuances of language. Students have to infer the connotation of the words they read: for example, the word *tough* could be used in both a positive and negative way. *"He's been through a lot but he's a tough guy." "It's been a tough day."* And what about interpreting the author's intention behind their words? Students might understand the literal meaning of *"Oh, life is tough!"* but context clues and tone might point to quite a different interpretation of those words. The English language also includes thousands of idioms: phrases or groups of words that have a meaning different from the literal meaning. *"He's over the moon." "Don't cry over spilled milk!" "She's feeling under the weather today." "What a tough cookie!"* Obviously, it is essential that we engage our students in discussions about context, tone, and connotation. These can sometimes be difficult to infer and your discussions will help build background knowledge and ultimately improve their understanding of the text they read.

Developing our students' reading comprehension is not a one-size-fits-all approach. Rather, it is an ongoing effort to understand their specific needs, support them with foundational skills, expose them to a variety of text, and teach explicit mini-lessons. The instructional practices in the upcoming sections provide effective structures to support student learning.

Instructional Practices to Support Reading

In Chapter 3, Pearson and Gallagher's *gradual release of responsibility* featured prominently. There are specific instructional practices to support reading at each stage of the gradual release of responsibility. Remember to look back to the sample weekly schedule (page 35) to see how each of these practices can be embedded into your week.

Read-Alouds

Read-alouds are a regular part of explicit instruction: *I do!* The role of read-alouds cannot be underestimated. As we discussed in the section on fluency, students need to hear effective, fluent reading. Sometimes, fluency may be the focus of the read-aloud, but even when it's not, students should hear you reading fluently every day. Read-alouds are used within our instruction to serve many other purposes too. They are opportunities for us to think-aloud, demonstrating the strategies of an effective reader. They are used to spark discussion or prompt reader response writing. Sometimes they are used to introduce a topic or concept in science or social studies. And often, read-alouds are used as mentor texts for writing as a way to examine the craft of a writer. Regardless of the lesson target, reading aloud to our students will expose them to a variety of genres of text, new vocabulary, and often text above their independent reading levels. Keep in mind, sometimes you will read aloud during language arts and sometimes in other subject areas.

I've noticed that some teachers choose to show videos of others reading books rather than reading to their class themselves. On occasion, if you don't have access to a physical copy of the book, this *might* be something to consider—but only if the reader is strong. In this context, students remain passive and there is little or no interaction. Showing a video of someone else reading takes away many instructional moves. In contrast, when an effective teacher reads aloud, they are able to ensure the experience is interactive, be responsive to students' understanding, and detect misconceptions that may arise. Consider the many instructional moves being made throughout a read-aloud: modelling something recently taught, talking-aloud, engaging students in various strategies, clarifying vocabulary or content, and relating to students' background knowledge. The reader on the screen certainly cannot do the same with your class.

Showing a video to your class as an extra—as a lunch activity, for example—is very different than using the video for instruction.

Shared Reading

During shared reading, you and your students read together: *We do!* A morning message is a daily opportunity for shared reading. The reading of a decodable book during phonics instruction is another. Shared reading is most effective when students can easily see the text, such as when it is projected on an interactive whiteboard. You may read to the students first and then invite them to read along with you. Within this structure, you are still able to provide support as needed, but you can also gauge the readiness and proficiency of your students and therefore be responsive, releasing more responsibility onto them as appropriate. Look for opportunities for shared reading throughout the day. For example, you might have an informational text projected for students during your science lesson. Consider reading it to them first, so they can hear you read it fluently and then talk about the vocabulary and content. After some discussion, ask students to read the text *with* you. Rereading the text will support their comprehension but it is also an opportunity to practice reading more difficult text with your support.

Guided Reading

Where shared reading is effective with the whole class, guided reading provides a structure to target skills with a specific group of students: *We do!*

What does guided reading look like?

Chapter 9: Supporting Literacy Success for All includes more information for dealing with students who require additional literacy support.

While you work with a small group, the majority of the class should be engaged in another productive task such as literacy stations, independent reading, or reader response writing. This gives you the chance to reinforce or teach a concept or strategy needed by only a small group of students. Keep guided reading sessions to a reasonable length: 15-20 minutes is typically enough. If you go beyond that timeframe, ensuring that the time is productive for the whole class may become challenging. Plan carefully and set your students up for success. Do not have the group engaged in something they've never done before or you are sure to be bombarded with questions and the time will not be effective for anyone.

Although you may want to work with all students in this context, be sure to prioritize. Spend more time in this context with students who need support with skills that are not at grade level. And keep in mind, there is no need to establish guided reading groups which stay consistent throughout the year. I prefer keeping the groups dynamic, changing them based on who needs support with a particular skill. Through observations and anecdotal notes, keep track of which students need support in which area. If four or five students need support with attending to punctuation, for example, or using titles and headings to improve comprehension, it is not necessary for these students to be at the same reading level. During the guided reading lesson, provide each student with a book at their independent or instructional level. Reinforce the skill with the whole group but then have each student practice with their own book. Listen to one student reading out loud (while the others practice reading their text silently) and support that student as needed. Then, move to the next individual. There is often a misconception that students should be listening to each other read during this time. For a much more efficient use of time, they should each practice on their own. Remember, guided reading is another opportunity to release more responsibility to the students and provide scaffolding as needed. When writing about guided reading, Routman (2014) says,

> … we need to be cautious about providing too much support, such as spending too much time on prereading activities or giving students all the "answers" so that we wind up doing most of the reading work. (132)

Think of this context as an opportunity for students to take calculated risks and practice in a smaller, less threatening environment.

Paired Reading/Reading Buddies

Paired reading, sometimes referred to as partner reading, releases responsibility onto the students a little more: *You do it together!* Unlike the previous instructional practices, you as the teacher are no longer present to provide support. Students are now practicing with their peers.

This is a structure that works well within the reading literacy station. Providing clear instructions on task cards will help ensure the time spent reading with a partner is used effectively. Direct students to practice something specific you have been working on: reading dialogue with appropriate phrasing and expression, or a particular comprehension strategy, such as making connections.

You may also consider another option for paired reading: reading buddies. Connect with another class in your school to establish cross-grade partners. Meet regularly—every two weeks or once a month—so students develop a relationship with their buddy. It doesn't really matter the grade levels that are paired, but with your colleague, take the time to ensure that the partners are a logical fit. You wouldn't want to pair a strong reader in the younger grade with a student not as confident from the older grade. Also, be intentional about how the time is used. On occasion, I have seen this structure misused. For some teachers, it simply becomes time for socializing with their colleague: if students see teachers using the time this way, they may do the same. It's not that the social component isn't valued. In fact, often these buddies form meaningful relationships. When the buddies react excitedly when they see each other in the hall, the importance of the relationship becomes obvious. But in order to value instructional time, be sure to set a learning focus. Present the time with reading buddies as a chance to "show off" newly learned skills. Before students meet with their buddy, have them practice what they are going to read. Remind them what you want them to "show off." In fact, ask them to explain to their buddy what they are going to demonstrate. For example, if the focus for the Grade 1 students has been using punctuation to guide their reading, these are some examples of what they might say to their buddies before they begin reading: "We've been practicing stopping at the periods." "We use punctuation like street signs to guide our reading." "We can read more fluently when we pay attention to punctuation." This is a way for them to articulate what they have been learning and sets a very specific focus for the time with their buddy. It also gives the buddies something specific to compliment.

If you teach the older grade of the reading buddy pairing, ask your students to choose a book from the library that they will read to their buddy. Encourage them to get to know interests, topics, and authors that their buddies enjoy. Ensure they have an opportunity to practice reading the book before they read to their buddy: remind them that they are modelling reading behaviors and that their little buddies look up to them.

I use reading buddies as a way to practice oral language skills, too. The students and I talk about how to connect with our buddies: what we could say to begin, what is polite, what we might say when the time is finished.

Although most of the time with buddies is spent reading, there may be other opportunities to connect with the other class throughout the year. Perhaps the younger class is doing an art project or a science experiment that the older buddies could help with. Perhaps the reading buddies become an authentic audience for something students have written. The entire class may become our audience for choral reading or readers' theatre!

Independent Reading

The ultimate goal of teaching students to read is so they can do so independently. Independent reading provides the opportunity to practice everything you have been teaching: *You do it alone!* We have already spent considerable time talking about independent reading in both Chapters 1 and 3. This important practice should be built into your daily timetable. Although you will provide at-level books when students are practicing within your instruction, independent reading is the opportunity for students to choose what they'd like to read. As Kate Roberts (2018) says, "When kids get to choose their own books, they read more" (17). We know that there are students who won't read at all if they are not reading in our classrooms. Carving out the time is important but we want to ensure the time is actually spent reading.

Over the years, I've noticed students who choose books that they *think* they should be reading based on what their peers are reading. Sadly, for some of these students, the books are much too challenging. If they choose a novel just because that's what they see others reading, but then engage in fake reading behavior, the time is not effective at all. I talk openly with my students about our uniqueness: we all have different interests, strengths, and abilities. I do not tolerate comments or behavior that is judgmental. We support each other. For our reluctant readers especially, creating a safe environment of trust and respect is essential. When choosing books, I remind students not to be concerned about others but to think about *themselves* as readers. I encourage each student to look for something they are *interested* in but also something they are *capable* of reading. If they choose a book on airplanes because they are interested in airplanes, they don't necessarily have to read every word on the page, but we do want them to be able to read at least some of the content. It may be somewhat above their independent level, but if they are motivated, they will read what they can. When I remind students of the importance of reading (perhaps even sharing the stats about time spent reading from page 36), they tend to understand why it is important to choose a book they can read, at least in part.

Interest Inventories

It doesn't take long to get to know your readers: those who read during every spare minute, those who enjoy it once they start, those who avoid it at all costs. From the day I meet my students, I work hard to help them identify as readers and entice them to read—calling them readers, having them create a heart map, having each of them develop a personal reading list. I also give my students an *interest inventory* near the beginning of the year to help me understand their interests. You may find some versions online, or you could create one yourself. A few revealing questions:

- What is your favorite thing to do?
- What games or sports do you enjoy? Do you play them or watch?
- What is your favorite movie? Why do you like it?
- Do you have a special talent or topic that you know a lot about?
- If you could learn more about any topic, what would it be?
- What is your favorite book? Why do you like it?
- Who is your favorite author? What do you like about their books?
- What are your favorite genres of books? (Consider listing options for students and letting them circle their favorites.)
- If you could go anywhere, where would you go?

I often use what I've learned in the interest inventories to engage my student writers too.

When I give the interest inventory to students, I read the questions aloud and give them time to complete the questions. There is no need for complete sentences in a task such as this as the goal is to learn about my students. After reading the completed interest inventories initially, I keep them on file. Then, if I notice a student not engaged during independent reading or taking a long time to choose a book, I look back to their responses to help me find a book I think they'd get excited about. For the student who loves to cook, I'll find a kid's cookbook. For the student obsessed with classical music, I'll find a biography about a composer. An animal lover? *National Geographic* has books at all levels. I see it as my mission to find books that every student in my class will enjoy reading!

When creating your weekly schedule, be sure to find 15-20 minutes each day for independent reading. Why?

> Practice, practice, and more practice will help students develop the fluency they need to read successfully. If you want to improve as a skier, a driver, a dancer, a singer—or anything else, really—it takes practice (Bright 2021, 84).

Independent reading is well worth the time. For added benefits, ask students to turn-and-talk to a partner for a minute or two at the end of independent reading. On a given day, you might simply ask them to talk about what they were reading. If you had requested that they practice a specific skill, ask them to talk about the skill they were practicing. If you had asked them to pay attention to new vocabulary, ask them to share what they found. On another day, ask them to read aloud a passage they enjoyed! Keep both the intentionality of your lessons and the joy of reading entrenched in this process each and every day.

What should you be doing during independent reading?

Read! At the beginning of the year, especially, read when your students are reading. Set an example so students can see sustained reading in action. What should you read? Anything! It might be a book of adult fiction or a nonfiction book that's part of a book study with your colleagues, perhaps it's a cookbook, a magazine, or a book from your classroom library. Really, it doesn't matter what. But as I mentioned earlier in the chapter, my junior high teacher friend says the book she's reading often sparks conversations. Students will see you as a reader when you read along with them. If you haven't read for pleasure recently, this might just help you get back into (or develop) the habit.

After a few weeks, once a routine has been established for independent reading, take the opportunity to *slide in beside* a student and engage in a short reading conference. Listen to the student read for a few minutes (whatever book they happen to have) and then ask them to retell that portion of the book. By asking them to explain what they've read—before you ask specific questions—you will likely get a better understanding of their comprehension. Sometimes, the questions you ask may prompt realizations or understanding that students hadn't thought about on their own. Questions can certainly be useful in getting them to think more deeply about the text, but initially, ask for a retell. These short conferences might reveal skills that you'd like to target during instruction, as well as give you a sense of their engagement, and whether or not they are choosing books at a reasonable level.

I understand that classroom life is hectic. I've lived it. Regardless, avoid the temptation of using independent reading for tasks such as collecting field trip forms or grading student work. If you use your time this way, students may perceive independent reading time as an extra or, worse, a time filler. Divide your time during independent reading between reading yourself and supporting individual students with their reading.

Okay… I know I've said "anything" but choose a print book or e-reader rather than reading from your phone, tablet, or computer. Students may assume you're doing something else if you're on another device!

Anecdotal Notes

Even though these *slide in beside* reading conferences are informal, jot down a few notes to keep track of what you notice. Some years, for easy reference, I created a page for each student and then always wrote my notes about that student on the same page. Other years, I used a scribbler or notebook and kept my notes chronological. Experiment to see what works best for you.

When making notes, consider the reading behaviors or strategies that you notice your students using (or not using). These notes can be helpful when writing comments for report cards. You may also want to note topics or authors they seem interested in.

Reading Assessments

Some schools or districts mandate formal reading assessments for students. For example, in the not-too-distant past, many districts mandated benchmark assessments for every student multiple times per year. Although the intentions were good, the significant amount of time spent on assessments took away from instructional time. With older students, benchmark assessments can take anywhere between 15-60 minutes per student. Imagine the amount of time spent assessing all 25 or 30 students in the class—two or three times a year! In these situations, I noticed that many teachers completed the assessments to fulfill the requirements of their school or district, but didn't use the information gathered to inform their instruction.

Can we still use benchmark assessments to assess student reading? If you have identified students who you deem at-risk, these assessments may help you learn more about the type of support they need and therefore guide your instruction or intervention. Thankfully, there are other methods of reading assessment that we can use to help us understand our readers that don't take quite so long. Consider the use of both informal running records and reading screeners.

Running Records

Running records are one component of benchmark assessments. In that context they are more formalized. I often take quick, informal running records during my reading conferences. How? As I listen to my students read, I make a check for each word they read correctly, note the errors they are making, and how often they self correct. If it is a text of their choosing, I know that the level may be beyond their own independent reading level but it gives me a sense of the difficulty of the text they have chosen. If I want to be more precise and determine a specific reading level, I use levelled books for the running records. Note the standard accuracy rates used for running records:

Independent: 95–100%
Instructional: 90–94%
Frustrational: 89% and below

For more information about running records, check with a district consultant or literacy coach. Also remember, the running record only provides one piece of the puzzle. We also want to determine our students' comprehension of the text through both a retell and questioning.

Reading Screeners

Reading screeners are being used more regularly in classrooms because they are much quicker to administer as compared to benchmark assessments. In fact, some screeners can be given to the whole class at the same time. These universal screeners are designed to identify students at risk for learning difficulties, in this case related to reading. Your province, district, or school may have specific screeners that you are asked to use (sometimes multiple times per year) to help monitor progress. If you are not directed to use a specific screener, consider the skill(s) you want to screen: phonemic awareness, word reading, oral reading fluency, and/or comprehension. These are a few of the most common:

- Acadience Reading (formally DIBELS: Dynamic Indicators of Basic Early Literacy Skills)
- PAST (the Phonological Awareness Screening Test)
- LeNS (the Letter Name–Sound test)
- CC3 (the Castles and Coltheart 3; assesses word reading)
- CTOPP-2 (Comprehensive Test of Phonological Processing)
- TOWRE (Test of Word Reading Efficiency)
- TOSWRF (Test of Silent Word Reading Fluency)
- TOSREC (Test of Silent Reading Efficiency and Comprehension)

Willms and Alberti (2022) suggest: "An effective screen should be quick and targeted, taking no more than ten to fifteen minutes per student" (23).

Some of the screeners listed above are free to use. Others are sold as a kit. *Assessing Reading: Multiple Measures* by Linda Diamond and B.J. Thorsnes also includes various tests targeting phonological awareness, decoding and word recognition, spelling, reading fluency, vocabulary, and comprehension to help determine student needs. In their book *This Is How We Teach Reading … And It's Working!*, Heather Willms and Giacinta Alberti (2022) provide a number of simple screeners that can be used with Kindergarten to Grade 3 students. You might also want to consider using a screening tool with students in older grades who are struggling to determine what support they need.

Keep in mind that screening tools are not meant as a summative assessment to be reported to parents. They help us identify who is at risk and determine the type of instruction and/or intervention that is required.

Re-examining Traditional Practices

Have you heard the story about the little girl watching her mom cook a ham for a special occasion?

"Mom why do you cut the ends off the ham before you cook it?"

"I'm not sure why, it's just what I learned from watching Grandma!"

The little girl turns to Grandma and says, "Grandma, why do you cut the ends off the ham before you cook it?"

"Hmmm… that's what my mother taught me. Something about soaking up the juices, I think. Why don't you call Great Grandma and ask her?"

In hearing the question, Great Grandma laughs. "Oh sweetie! I used to cut the ends off because I never had a pan big enough for the whole ham!"

This story, of which many versions have been told, reminds us to consider *why* we do what we do. Are we teaching a particular way because it's the way we were taught, or because it's what we see going on next door? If so, there's a chance that our practices are not grounded in strong pedagogy. Reflecting on our purpose and considering our students' best interests is essential. This section is not intended to be judgmental but to prompt us to reflect on our current practices to ensure they are effective for students.

Round-Robin Reading

I'm sure you experienced round-robin reading as a student at some point in your education. It has been a common choice—across subject areas—when teachers want a particular text read aloud. You remember: one student reads while the rest of the class is supposed to follow along and listen. Then the next person reads and so on. In my experience, it was often student by student, row by row. I remember counting ahead, trying to figure out which paragraph I would be asked to read out loud. (I was nervous and I was a proficient reader. Imagine those who were not confident or competent with the level of text.) Was I engaged in what the other readers were reading? Not at all. At first, I was determining what I would read; once I had my turn reading, why pay attention any longer?

What does round-robin reading accomplish? Probably not what teachers expect. After all, most students are not usually engaged in the content and many are distracted and nervous about reading aloud. Are students getting practice by reading aloud one paragraph? Not a lot. Certainly not enough. Given the amount of time on the activity as a whole, each student is reading very little.

If our goals are to help students comprehend the content of the text, and practice their reading, there are many instructional practices that are much more effective. By reading aloud (and thinking aloud) to students, we can model effective reading, and involve students in turn-and-talk opportunities to help them construct meaning about the content. The same would be true for shared reading. We might read some of the text to students and then invite them to read some of the text with us. There is no need to put one student on the spot. We might also consider asking students to read the text with a partner. This situation is much more comfortable for students and the proportion of time spent reading is significantly greater. Utilize these instructional practices—read-alouds, shared reading, partner reading—in all subject areas! They should not be saved for the language arts classroom. Good practice is good practice.

Reading Logs

Reading logs are often used to track minutes or pages read. Sometimes they are used to record reading in school, sometimes at home, sometimes both. They are seen as a measure of accountability, proof that students are reading. But consider this: If students are reading in front of you, you have the proof you need and you can detect fake readers in the process. If they're reading at home, is the log a true reflection of time spent reading? We don't really know. Some students are asked to get a parent signature next to the recorded minutes, but again there is no guarantee that the parents actually saw their child reading. I've also seen situations where teachers insisted that students get a parent to sign their log each day, and it became problematic and stressful for some. Unfortunately, not all of our students have engaged and available parents; some live in challenging circumstances where a parent signature is much less important than finding food for dinner or taking care of younger siblings. Knowing our students and understanding their circumstances can help us be proactive and maintain their dignity.

Consider which provides more opportunity to improve reading and comprehension. One student reading and 25 listening? Or 13 students reading and 13 listening?

Ultimately, my goal is to motivate students to read as much as possible. If I have students who read willingly and voraciously, the log will not likely motivate them further. If I do have some students who are motivated by recording the time or pages read (like me with my fitness tracker), then yes, let them keep track! But avoid making this a blanket expectation. Spend the energy finding engaging, relevant books for them to read.

Incentive Programs (School-Wide or Classroom-Based)

I have been in many schools with incentive programs for reading. The goal? Get students reading! These incentive programs often have a minute-goal for individual readers or for the class. When the goal is reached, students earn a reward of some kind. What could possibly be wrong with this practice? Willingham (2017) offers this perspective,

> Rewards do work, at least in the short term. If you find a reward that the child cares about, he will read in order to get it. The problem is that you don't get the attitude boost we've predicted. In fact, the attitude is often less positive because of the reward. (149)

Miller (2009) concurs:

> Unfortunately, the only purpose these programs serve is to convince students there is no innate value in reading and that it is only worth doing if there is a prize attached. (150)

Some teachers adore their reward programs and are convinced that the results are positive. As Willingham suggests, they may be *at first*. Unfortunately, I have witnessed students who reach their weekly or monthly goal and say, "I'm done reading this month." They were reading merely for the reward and feel no desire to keep reading. It seems these students have not yet experienced the pleasure that comes from losing yourself in a good book or the thrill of learning something new through the books we read.

If our goal is to motivate students beyond the short term, there is so much we can do: surround them with quality books, find topics or genres they enjoy, generate book buzz by encouraging students, teachers, and all staff to talk about the books they are reading. This will be more effective in creating lifelong readers. A pizza lunch, not so much.

Whole-Class Novel Studies

The whole-class novel study is yet another area where the pendulum seems to swing in favor or out. Think of experiences you had as a student. I would guess that, in one grade or another, you were reading the same novel as the rest of your class. Were you *able* to read the book? *Did* you read the book? Do you think *all* of your classmates were able to access the words on the page? As an avid reader, I quite enjoyed these experiences, but it didn't occur to me that some of my peers might be intimated by the process and experience frustration. In a traditional novel study, students of all abilities are asked to read the same book with little or no differentiation or consideration for those who may struggle with the text. In this traditional model, there might also be pages of comprehension questions, quizzes on minute details, and round-robin reading. These novel studies often dragged on for weeks or months at a time. When outlined in this way, pedagogically, the concerns become obvious.

And yet, I fondly remember specific moments of emotion and impassioned participation with my own classes when discussing *Charlotte's Web*, *Island of the Blue Dolphins*, *The Giver*, *The Miraculous Journey of Edward Tulane*, and *The One and Only Ivan*. These conversations wouldn't have occurred had we not all been reading the same book. Through shared reading experiences, students gain exposure to diverse texts or genres they might not choose on their own. Often, our community of learners is strengthened, providing us with common realizations and reference points throughout the school year. Students and teacher will journey together through difficult content and sometimes difficult text. Students will share their own interpretations and opinions, often pushing the thinking of their peers. When executed well, the reading of a shared novel can also provide many opportunities to improve oral language communication. Although Beers and Probst (2017) have reservations about a traditional novel study, they too see the benefits of everyone reading the same book:

> We love talking about it. We want to compare favorite passages or talk about parts that surprised us or ask each other questions about why a character did this or that. We like the community that is created as we share our reading. We like learning from one another…. Too much right now seems to be about dividing us. Don't we need some common experiences that unite us? Isn't the sharing of literature one of the most powerful ways to unite? (143–144)

The use of *literature circles* is an effective option for reading novels in the classroom context. Within this structure, small groups of students are each reading a different book. One of the benefits of this approach is that it may be easier to ensure that all students are reading at an appropriate level. The time within their groups is intentional with each student rotating through various roles. For more information, see Harvey Daniels's book *Literature Circles: Voice and Choice in Book Clubs & Reading Groups*.

"Having the support of a teacher and a class of peers when reading a book can lift the level of our thinking and can hold our attention in ways that sometimes reading on our own does not" (Roberts 2018, 11).

So it seems that it's not the shared reading of a novel that's the problem, it's the approach. And once again, if we default to the way we were taught, we might be doing our students a disservice. We want to avoid falling into the trap of a long, drawn-out traditional novel study, and instead find ways to make it accessible for all of our readers.

If you are planning a whole-class novel study, I recommend reading *A Novel Approach* by Kate Roberts before you begin. I will outline some of the important suggestions she makes, but she dives much deeper into both rationale and suggestions. If we recognize the problems with traditional novel studies, we can plan accordingly and avoid the pitfalls. One of the most serious concerns is that the text is likely too difficult for some of our students to read independently, and the very fact that it is novel-length is intimidating for those readers. When planning your novel study, consider how each chapter will be read ahead of time. Roberts suggests choosing a few parts of the book that you will read aloud to students (with them following in their copy). A good guideline: first and last chapters, and critical scenes. Then, decide which parts of the book students will read during class time and how. They can read some parts independently and some with a partner. While the class is reading in these contexts, you can provide support either in one-on-one conferences or guided reading groups for students who would benefit. Check in or confer daily with those who you know may struggle with the text. If you assign students to read parts of the book at home, assign the especially exciting parts—but nothing too long. To ensure that students are reading the book at the same pace, most of the book should be read in class.

One of the other concerns of a traditional novel study is the length of time it takes. Roberts (2017) reminds us that "Less is more: keep the pace brisk!" (52). With elementary students plan for about three weeks. How? Resist the temptation to analyze and talk about everything! Sometimes, yes, talk about the craft of the writer, but be careful that you're not analyzing every line of the book. That's when the drudgery sets in. In fact, Roberts suggests that more than a focus on content, our mini-lessons during a novel study should focus on skills: self-monitoring, fluency, inferring, making connections, annotating text, etc. To help students understand what they are reading, consider the strategies you use in other contexts: talk time and reader response writing, for example.

A whole-class novel study can be an incredible experience when led intentionally and when every student is supported with the text. Even still, it is one instructional practice and shouldn't be used at the exclusion of others.

Although the teaching of reading may be daunting, it is also exciting to see students embrace the literate world. Our own words and actions can influence how students feel about reading—today and years from now. Consider this a marvellous opportunity!

7

Writing

"Writing, to me, is simply thinking through my fingers." — Isaac Asimov

Why Teach Writing?

The teaching of writing is my greatest passion. This chapter provides an overview of the writing forms and processes that you can use in your classroom. My first two books, *How Do I Get Them to Write?* and *Freewriting with Purpose,* go much deeper.

The teaching of writing is in the curriculum, yes. But just like reading, I want my students to understand that we are learning to write because writing is a skill they will use beyond the classroom. They are not learning to write for me, their teacher, they are learning to write because it is a relevant literacy skill that will help them in immeasurable ways—today and in the future. Although few of our students will grow up to be authors, the ability to write allows one to function more fully in the world. In Chapter 2, I suggested asking students to brainstorm the many things we read and have them create a page entitled Reading is Everywhere (see page 28). To set the context for writing, I ask students *why* we write: the purposes, functions, reasons. I let them discuss their ideas in a small group and record their ideas on chart paper. Then, I invite students to engage in a *gallery walk* where they can read the brainstorming by other groups. They are encouraged to return to their own page and add to their ideas based on what they noticed others had written. The whole-class discussion that follows helps students understand the many reasons we learn to write.

The beauty of teaching in an elementary classroom is that we have an opportunity to shape our students' views on writing. Simply assigning students written tasks is not going to give them a sense of empowerment or confidence with the complex skill of writing. The teaching of writing should be as intentional as the teaching of reading. I categorize the writing we do in our classroom in two ways: *learning to write* and *writing to learn*. Our curriculum can direct us to specific skills to teach when students are *learning to write*. In addition, our students should be *writing to learn*. As we discussed in Chapter 2, writing is a form of thinking. The information in this chapter will focus primarily on learning to write, writing that tends to occur in our language arts classrooms. The next chapter, Literacy in the Content Areas, addresses writing to learn to help students construct meaning through writing.

Writing Makes us Vulnerable

How do *you* feel about writing—do you enjoy it or dread it? Is it something you do only when you have to? How do you feel about sharing your writing with others?

I work with thousands of students each year as a writer-in-residence in schools. With each class, I begin by talking about what they like about writing and what they find challenging or dislike about it. In most classes, the conversation about what they like tends to be much shorter than what they find challenging or what they dislike! When discussing the challenges of writing, no matter the grade level, students share similar sentiments: *"I don't know how to spell." "I don't know what to say." "I don't want anyone to read my writing." "I'm not a good writer."* Sadly, many students are reluctant to write. In my experience, the higher the grade, the higher the proportion of reluctant writers. As we discussed with reading, writing too, is an emotional journey. The more positive the experience, the more inclined students will be to engage in the writing process. I endeavor to create joyful writers: writers with confidence, writers willing to take risks.

Imagine you were asked to write and submit your writing to your administrator each day. How would you feel? Probably the same as our students. Vulnerable. And what if that writing was going to be assessed by your administrator? Even more vulnerable. When we put words to paper, unavoidably we reveal all sorts of things about ourselves: our writing abilities, our weaknesses, our beliefs, our emotions, our circumstances. Writing is risk-taking. If our students are going to feel comfortable learning to write in our classrooms, our approach must be intentional. Yet again it becomes obvious why developing positive, trusting relationships with our students is essential.

Share your own fears and apprehensions when learning something new. By acknowledging the emotion tied to writing, we contribute to an environment where our students are more willing to take risks as writers.

Daily Writing Practice

If you look back at the sample weekly schedules in Chapter 3, you will notice daily opportunities to write. Much of the writing our students do occurs during language arts, but they should be writing in other subject areas as well. I divide the forms of writing into weekly writing opportunities and those that we focus on at particular times of the year. The weekly writing—as evident in the sample schedules—includes journal writing, freewriting, and reader response. These are easily embedded into the week and provide students with daily writing practice. These forms of writing are considered low-stakes writing: students understand that these opportunities provide writing practice and they are not worried about a looming assessment.

In my ongoing work with teachers, many have expressed the belief that they have to *assess* everything their students write. Others believe they have to *read* everything their students write. As you will see in this chapter, it is going to be much more effective if you don't. And really, if you believe you have to read and/or assess everything your students write, I guarantee your students won't be writing enough. By taking away the continual sharing and assessment of writing, we immediately reduce some of the stress and anxiety our students feel.

How often do your students currently write? As Natalie Goldberg (2014) suggests, "Like running, the more you do it, the better you get at it" (11).

Emergent Writers

Chapter 11 of *How Do I Get Them to Write?* delves deeper into supporting our emergent writers.

Although many older students share a reluctance to write, our emergent writers often share excitement about writing. As they learn the functions and possibilities that writing holds, they want to enter this world. We can capitalize on their excitement and provide them with skills and tools to ensure success. All of the work you do with the foundational skills of phonological awareness, phonemic awareness, and orthographic mapping will assist students with their writing. In addition, the tools set up in your classroom—such as a sound wall and a word wall—will empower student writers.

A general guideline: hold students accountable for words they are copying and for word-wall words. Accept the invented spelling of other words.

Initially, in Grade 1 in particular, I give students sentence starters for writing such as "I like…" or "I want…" Students copy these words (be sure to talk about capitalization and spacing) and then finish the sentence as they are able. Most emergent writers will not yet use conventional spelling as they finish the sentence, and that's okay. It they are writing words such as *ice cream*, *dolphins*, or *hockey*, they will use invented spelling based on their current phonemic knowledge. It is essential that we do not over-correct our students' attempts at writing. Over-correction tends to stifle student writers. Their perception when we over-correct is that they are not good writers and they will then be less willing to take risks. Instead, we need to celebrate their attempts. As you teach explicit phonics and morphology lessons, their ability to write with more conventional spelling will increase.

One other strategy worth reinforcing here is the use of oral language as a scaffold. After you share the sentence starter, discuss what students might write to finish the sentence. Let them share their ideas with a partner. Many students will decide what they want to write during the discussion and then they can concentrate more on encoding during the actual writing time.

I have been in Grade 1 classrooms where students do not start writing until months into the school year. The rationale by teachers: they don't yet have the foundational skills needed to write independently. My philosophy is quite the opposite: I literally begin on the first or second day of school. Scaffolded, of course. But get them writing! The sooner they begin, the sooner they will believe they are writers. Build skills, build confidence, and start early.

Learning to Write in Various Forms

Just as students need exposure to many genres of text, they also need practice writing in various forms. Three forms of writing—freewriting, journal writing, and reader response—will be integrated into our weekly schedules. The others—such as the writing of narratives, transactional writing, and poetry—will be included in our overall year plan, taught at specific times during the school year. Let's have a look at each.

Freewriting

My first book—*How Do I Get Them to Write?*—includes one chapter on freewriting. The response by teachers was so overwhelming, I wrote my second book—*Freewriting with Purpose*—entirely on this process and how it can be used effectively in our classrooms to get our students writing (and writing well) across the curriculum.

You have heard reference to freewriting throughout this book. Peter Elbow (1998) has said, "Freewriting is the easiest way to get words on paper and the best all-around practice in writing that I know" (13). I found this sentiment to be true for myself as a writer and I quickly realized that it could also be a powerful tool for students. I first introduced it to a Grade 6 class that I was teaching and it was immediately successful. Since then I have introduced it in hundreds of classrooms. The response from students and teachers is overwhelming. When introduced effectively, it breaks down barriers, reduces the reluctance to write, and brings joy to the writing process.

What is freewriting?

When I was experimenting with freewriting with elementary-age students, I referred to the work of Peter Elbow (who coined the term) and Natalie Goldberg. Freewriting is a short, timed session of continuous writing. The intent is to keep our pens or pencils moving across the paper the entire writing time. In theory, this might seem daunting to students but there are a few essential guidelines to ensure that students can—and do—write continuously. To support our elementary writers, I adapted the process slightly by creating a short prompt.

Guidelines for freewriting with students:

- Copy the prompt and write the first thing that comes to mind.
- Do not overthink the process or censor yourself.
- Do not worry about spelling, grammar, punctuation, or capitalization while you are writing. (You don't ignore it, but you don't worry about it.)
- There is no need to reference tools such as a dictionary or personal dictionary at this time. Writing time is writing time. We can always check our spelling later.
- You will always have the choice to share *all, some, or none* of your freewriting.
- If your brain stops and therefore your hand stops, rewrite the prompt and then continue writing whatever comes to mind.

As Peter Elbow said, it is *the easiest way to get words on paper*. Why? To begin, we've taken away one of the barriers that many students have articulated: spelling. Regardless of grade level, students often stop writing or resist writing if they don't know how to spell a word. We can remind them that spelling is important, but not during the process of freewriting. One of the other reasons freewriting is so successful is that students are given a choice of whether or not to share any given freewrite. They're not frozen by the thought: *My teacher is going to read this.* This reduces the anxiety that many students feel while writing and they learn not to overthink the process. As Elbow (1998) explains: "Sometimes, in fact, when people think too much during the early stages about what they want to end up with, that preoccupation with the final product keeps them from attaining it" (7). By giving students the choice to share, they worry less about the final product and are more likely to take risks. As Goldberg (2005) says in *Writing Down the Bones*:

> … the aim is to burn through to first thoughts, to the place where energy is unobstructed by social politeness or the internal censor, to the place where you are writing what your mind actually sees and feels, not what it *thinks* it should see or feel. (8-9)

I have found that a prompt is essential for student writers if they are to write continuously. Otherwise they just stop. Rewriting the prompt as needed tends to spark a next thought, giving students something else to write about. It doesn't matter if they begin writing about something different the second (or third) time they write the prompt because the goal is to write continuously. Will we create an organized, polished piece of writing during the writing time? Not likely. But remember, freewriting is not about the end *product*, it is about the *process*. Later, you will ask students to choose one of their freewrites to revise during a mini-lesson. But not every freewrite will end up at this stage; it's the very reason why freewriting is so powerful.

When we give a typical writing task, instead of writing continuously, students (and adults, for that matter) often stop to read what they've written throughout the process. This start-and-stop pattern often inhibits writers from going deeper. During freewriting, we avoid this by writing continuously—preventing us from overthinking and trying to be perfect with the draft. Paradoxically, even though we're less concerned about what we're writing, the writing is often more powerful: raw, deep, and real.

What do you do while your students are freewriting?

By writing alongside your students, you can relate to their experiences and discuss the writing process with more authenticity.

I encourage you to freewrite with your students, for many reasons. We've acknowledged that writing makes us vulnerable: students are much more willing to engage in the process when they see their teacher doing the same. It also ensures that students cannot ask you questions at this time: it's writing time for *everyone*, teacher included! This is useful in all grade levels, but our youngest writers tend to ask many questions during writing time, especially those that begin "How do you spell…?" By writing *with* them, students become used to taking risks and attempting to write words on their own rather than relying on our help. In addition to these benefits, you will learn a lot about the writing process that your students experience and be able to discuss it with them with both credibility and relatability. Later in the chapter, we will explore how to use existing freewrites during the teaching of specific skills.

How long do our students freewrite?

Can Grade 1 students learn to freewrite? Yes! I begin freewriting as early as January of Grade 1, depending on the group. Earlier in the year isn't realistic, but they can certainly begin in the second half of the year.

Although students may be initially intimidated by the idea of continuous writing, they are always both surprised and relieved when I explain that we will only write for six or seven minutes. This timeframe is manageable for students of all ages. Our youngest writers will take longer to physically form the letters and apply their phonic knowledge. Our older writers can actually write quite a lot during this short time. Although we could potentially push the timeframe longer once they are familiar with the process, I try not to go much beyond 10 to 12 minutes. I want to ensure success for *all* writers in the room. Yes, you have some writers that could keep going, but we want all students to enjoy and feel successful with the process.

Although you may put a timer visible for students to see in other contexts, I avoid this during freewriting as I find some students fixate on the timer. Instead, I use the stopwatch on my phone and count up. This enables me to monitor the time and read the room. If I notice students slowing down within the first few minutes, I give the class a reminder: *"Remember, write the first thing that comes to mind. Don't overthink it."* If we're getting close to the end of six minutes and I notice some students beginning to slow down, I might say, *"Okay, Grade 2 writers, let's push through for one more minute."* If at six minutes, everyone is still writing furiously, I might push it another minute or two before I give a last-minute warning: *"Okay, Grade 4 writers, finish the sentence you are on and quietly read your writing."* This is a routine I establish during the first freewrite and students are respectful of this quiet time to read their work, most likely because they're curious to read what they've written. Even though the writing time is short, by the time I read it afterwards, I too, am often surprised by what I wrote.

Take the time needed to be intentional the first time you ask your class to freewrite. To ensure a positive experience, explain the process thoroughly and establish routines from the beginning. The time you invest upfront will ensure that freewriting becomes a powerful tool in your classroom.

Journal Writing

I have strong, positive feelings about journal writing in schools because of my own experiences as a student. When I was in junior high, my language arts teacher had us write in what he called our Weekend Update. We wrote every Monday and he wrote back to us each week. This experience became much more than writing for me: it was therapeutic and life-giving, a way of coping. My father had been recently diagnosed with multiple sclerosis and my grandmother had died a few months prior. Although I assume most students were writing about their weekends, I was using this journal to process the changes in my life with the support of a trusted adult. I looked forward to this time and discovered a whole new purpose to writing. Looking back now, I assume that I was not the only student who found this writing to be a coping mechanism.

When I became a teacher, I began to use journal writing with my own students—at all grade levels. I decided to begin the week with this routine. Each Monday, students know they will have the opportunity to share with me through writing and I will write back to each of them. And although it is another opportunity for writing practice, to me, it is also a way to connect with each of my students: to get to know their interests, their circumstances, and their struggles when they trust me enough to share them.

As I explained in Chapter 3, I put my students' journals on their desks before they arrive on Monday morning. Most students eagerly anticipate my response from last week and are excited to come into the class and begin the week. With older students, there is no instruction required; they simply begin writing. With Grade 1 (and sometimes Grade 2) students, I give a topic or prompt and then engage them in a discussion to ensure they have an idea of what to write about before they begin the process of encoding. I also ask my Grade 1 and 2 students to raise their hand when they finish writing. I then go to their desk or table and ask them to read me what they wrote. It is important that they get into the habit of reading over their work after they finish and, because they are reading to me, I can ask for clarification and provide in-the-moment feedback. If I notice a word-wall word spelled incorrectly, I remind the student to fix the spelling before handing it in. If the student hasn't used proper spacing or punctuation, I can guide them at this time. I don't comment on everything, but I choose one or two timely things to help them form good habits and ultimately improve their communication. I always do so respectfully, valuing their attempts. This is timely, differentiated support for our youngest student writers.

This powerful tool for connection should be honored as such. Other than the oral suggestions I give to my youngest writers when they read their entry out loud, I do not correct my students' journal writing. If student journals are "marked up" by the teacher, students often feel deflated because we seem to be highlighting their mistakes. Although likely well-intentioned, correcting our students' journal entries gives the message that we're more interested in proper conventions rather than the content of their message. By taking the time to write a short response in each students' journal, we value their words and forge connections. Our responses are brief: one or two sentences is usually enough.

It is important that our students understand *why* we do what we do, including why we write in various forms. I am transparent about my own experiences with journal writing and explain that this type of writing is a way to explore emotion, and is also a way for us to connect, teacher to student.

Although I rarely ask students in Grades 3 and up to read me their journal entry before handing it in, I train all students to read their writing to themselves and correct any mistakes they come across.

Sometimes, I might even pose a question that might prompt next week's writing. Consider the purpose of journal writing and think back to Adam Grant's words: "It's about fostering a culture that allows all students to grow intellectually and thrive emotionally" (176). By connecting with our students through journal writing, we begin to understand the complexity of each individual, ultimately building a stronger relationship with each student.

Reader Response

When we consider the strands of language, reading and writing are typically written as a pair. They are flip sides of the same coin, if you will. Pam Allyn describes the relationship between the two beautifully: "Reading is like breathing in; writing is like breathing out." When I engage students in a discussion after a read-aloud, I often hear the same three or four voices providing responses. And yet, I want all students to have the opportunity to share their insights and connections to what we read on a regular basis.

Although we may all read the same text, our responses and interpretations will be different according to our own prior knowledge and experiences. Louise Rosenblatt—highly regarded for her reading research and its influence on pedagogy—called this the Reader Response Theory, or the Transactional Theory. She suggested that a transaction occurs between the reader and a text: the reader constructs meaning from both the words on the page and also from their prior experiences and knowledge.

I include reader response writing on our weekly schedule. Once set up, it doesn't take much time but it is a powerful way for students to connect with text. Think about the many learning opportunities before they even begin to write: we are reading aloud, thinking aloud, and talking about the text and the author's intent. During this form of writing, the books become the springboard. Best of all, I find that once students have learned to freewrite, they approach reader response writing in a similar way. They understand that their writing doesn't have to be perfect, it's just about getting their ideas on the page. They can always return to the writing afterwards to fix any errors they made.

As with freewriting, I find that this process works best when students are given prompts. In this case, I provide a choice of prompts to ensure that all students can connect to the text in some way. The prompts fall into two main categories: a *reaction* to the text (*I noticed…*, *I liked the part when…*, *I was confused about…*) and a *connection* to their own life (*I am thinking about…*, *I feel…*, *This reminds me of…*). When given a choice of two or three prompts, students may choose to use only one or they may move between the choices you've given. If I have read the picture book *A Family Is a Family Is a Family* to my students, I might put three prompts on the board for students to choose from: *I noticed…*, *My family…*, and *Families…*. These particular prompts enable our students to react to the book, connect with their own situation, or both.

In *Disrupting Thinking*, Beers and Probst (2017) explain the Book, Head, Heart (BHH) framework as a type of reader response. Sometimes, I use this framework to guide my students' writing. Again, I use prompts to scaffold their writing. For example, the first paragraph begins with the prompt *In this book…* and students then describe *what's in the book*. The second paragraph begins with *I am thinking…* and explains *what's in my head*. The third paragraph begins with *I feel…* and describes *what's in my heart*.

My first book—*How Do I Get Them to Write?*—has a chapter dedicated to each form of writing.

Reader response writing is another form of low-stakes writing providing a way to connect with what has been read as well as another form of writing practice.

Adapt this process for younger students by having them write three sentences rather than three paragraphs.

I introduce reader response writing as early as Kindergarten. One of my favorite books to use with Kindergarten students is *Hug Machine* by Scott Campbell. After reading the book to students, we talk about our *reactions* to the book: favorite parts and parts that made us laugh. (There are many!) Then, we talk about our *connections* to the book: *"Who do you like to hug? Who do you know that gives good hugs?"* After our discussion, I provide students with a blank page and I ask them to *write* about the book. My Kindergarten students would be familiar with the idea that books communicate messages through both pictures and words. This understanding is important when they begin their own *writing*. I never assume that Kindergarten students will only draw pictures. Some may copy the word *hug* or another word I have taken the time to encode on the board, some may write a few letters, others may add words they know such as *mom, dad,* or a sibling's name. Some may even be able to string a short sentence together: *I hug my mom.*

On occasion, I have heard teachers share that they consider reader response writing as an extra and not a necessity. I invite you to consider your curricular outcomes. Besides the relevant writing outcomes, most provinces also have outcomes asking students to respond to text. For example, in Nova Scotia, one of the outcomes in the Language Arts Curriculum is: *Learners will respond personally and critically to a range of culturally diverse texts.* The indicators under this outcome for primary students include drawing pictures (or pictures with labels and/ or text) about their personal reactions. In the older grades, the expected responses become more complex. In the Ontario Language Curriculum, strand *C3. Critical Thinking in Literacy*, includes many expectations that can be addressed through reader response.

"What text should I choose to elicit effective reader response writing?"

Most often I use picture books for this purpose. However, it is also effective to engage students in reader response during the reading of a novel. As for topic, think back to Chapter 6 and our reference to Dr. Rudine Sims Bishop's essay entitled "Mirrors, Windows, and Sliding Glass Doors." We can choose books with a universal element that students can relate to in some way: hugs, home, family, pets, or loss, for example. These books may act as mirrors and student often share interesting observations or reflections. We can also take this opportunity to choose books that will be windows, exposing students to diverse experiences, places, and cultures. The writing after reading these texts is often enlightening. By looking at your curriculum, you can be even more deliberate about choosing texts and text forms that help meet your outcomes.

What about assessment?

I do not assess most of my students' reader response writing. On occasion, I may ask students to submit their writing to give me an idea of their comprehension and the connections they are making related to curricular outcomes. I make it clear that I am not assessing the writing itself. Even still, I always give students an opportunity to revise and edit anything they hand in.

Narrative Writing

"We are all human; we all have stories to tell" (Routman 2024, 37).

Why narrative writing? I have been asked this question by many teachers over the years. Consider this: as an elementary teacher, how many days have you gone without reading your students a story? For most of us, the answer is minuscule.

As Madeleine L'Engle says, "Stories make us more alive, more human, more courageous, more loving." Some of my most cherished moments as a teacher are those surrounding the sharing of a good story: the emotion and the discussion that follows. Thomas Newkirk (2023) says, "It is impossible to imagine social interactions without the attraction of storytelling. Our very identity is built on our life stories" (103). It's true: humans connect through story. Your colleagues enter the staffroom at recess with stories to tell… your students enter your classroom with stories to tell… and we head home at the end of each day with stories to tell. Narrative stories engage most students. We can capitalize on this engagement to help them become more confident readers and writers.

I realize that reading stories is not the same as telling stories or writing stories. But have you noticed that you understand something better when you have to teach it? Why is that? When you know you have to teach something, you give the topic or concept more thought, construct your own meaning, and find a way to best explain it. The same could be said for storytelling. By writing narratives, we are forced to think more about the elements of story and the techniques used by authors. In doing so, we ultimately become stronger readers. Our comprehension improves and we become more aware of what we are reading and how it was created. In teaching our students to write narratives, we explore the elements of story within countless mentor texts. Examining mentor texts for any element—a plot pattern, dialogue, character, setting, effective beginnings—will support student understanding. We have to make sense of various intersecting elements in order to tell a story.

For specific information about each of the plot patterns, and a graphic organizer for each, see Chapter 6 of *How Do I Get Them to Write?*

Unlike the forms of writing discussed thus far, I find students benefit from a structure for writing narratives. Near the beginning of my teaching career, I attended an in-service led by JoAnne Moore who introduced me to the idea of **plot patterns**. I also encounter this concept frequently when I read books for aspiring fiction writers. What are plot patterns? Put simply, they are the common pattern or structure of a story. I focus on five plot patterns with elementary students: transformation stories, stuck stories, circle stories, competition stories, and quest stories. When students begin to recognize the patterns in the stories they read, it becomes much easier for them to organize and write their own stories.

Although we are *reading* narratives each and every week, the *writing* of narratives is spread throughout the year. On the sample year plan on page 33, narrative writing is introduced in November. This is when I typically introduce transformation stories because so many Christmas or holiday stories follow this pattern. By introducing the weekly, low-stakes forms of writing during the first few months of school, we are able to establish a mindset towards writing, one in which students are willing to take risks. Most students will carry this mindset into their narrative writing and be less intimidated by the form. I revisit narrative writing a few times throughout the year with a different plot pattern and focus each time. For example, if I teach transformation stories in November and December, I might pair this plot pattern with a focus on character and dialogue. Perhaps I revisit narrative writing in February. This time I may teach stuck stories and focus on effective story beginnings. Of course, students are encouraged to apply what they previously learned about character and dialogue too. And finally, in May, I might introduce quest stories and pair this plot pattern with a focus on setting.

Enjoy the reading and writing of stories in your elementary classroom. Students are likely learning more than you realize.

Transactional Writing

Transactional writing includes a variety of nonfiction text forms.

Most of our students will not write narratives outside of our classrooms, but they will write to communicate in other ways. Transactional writing is viewed as more functional—nonfiction writing to persuade, enlighten, or inform. Under the umbrella of transactional writing, consider these forms: letter writing (for older students, business-style emails), opinion pieces, persuasive writing, expository text, procedural text, and articles. Your curricular documents may specify the form or indicate the function of the writing through the language used. Consider the following outcomes from various provincial curriculum. What type of writing does each suggest?

Note: Most language arts curriculum is developed as a spiral. If you see an outcome from your province on this list but not at your grade level, there is a likely similar outcome at your grade level.

- Draft short, simple texts of various forms and genres, including personal narratives, persuasive texts, and procedural texts, using a variety of media, tools, and strategies. (Ontario Language: Grades 1 and 2)
- Sequence sections of writing in a logical order. (Alberta English Language Arts and Literature: Grade 3)
- Use strategies in writing and other ways of representing to discover and express personal attitudes, feelings, and opinions. (Nova Scotia English Language Arts: Grade 4)
- Create written and media texts, collaboratively and independently, in different modes (expressive, transactional, and poetic), and in an increasing variety of forms. (Nova Scotia English Language Arts: Grade 5)
- Write to inform, explain, describe, or report for a variety of purposes and audiences. (Alberta English Language Arts and Literature: Grade 5)
- Students will be expected to create texts collaboratively and independently, using a variety of forms for a range of audiences and purposes—demonstrate understanding that particular forms require the use of specific features, structures and patterns. (Newfoundland and Labrador English Language Arts: Grade 6)

"Giving unreal writing activities to our students is about as useful as giving occupational therapy for stroke victims to people who are in perfect health." — Mem Fox (1993, 4)

As with narrative writing, I spread transactional forms of writing throughout the year as shorter units of study. We certainly don't need to write letters all year long, but a short exploration of the form and function is important. Whenever possible, I try to make the writing experiences as authentic as possible. Letters written to thank a guest speaker or host for a field trip, letters to ask for donations, letters to a city councillor, letters to Santa, or even a pen pal, all provide a genuine audience for our students. As a twist, a Grade 3 teacher I know had her students write letters to the Grinch and no surprise, they loved it! And, just as we spoke of using mentor texts for narrative writing, our students need to see examples of each type of text we ask them to write.

Poetry

Not all teachers have positive associations with poetry and some avoid sharing the form with students. And yet, poetry can be a wonderful opportunity to engage in both the playfulness and power of language. Challenge yourself to find poems that you and your students will all enjoy.

Although we read poetry throughout the year, the writing of poetry will be more limited. I try to be intentional about exposing my students to at least one poem each week. Choose the initial poems carefully to ensure students are captivated by the form. Nicola Davies, Dennis Lee, Kenn Nesbitt, Jack Prelutsky, Shel Silverstein, and Jane Yolen write enjoyable and accessible poetry for children. Don't feel the need to analyze the poems, especially at the beginning. Just read and enjoy. As the year goes on, begin to talk about specific techniques used by the writer. By sharing the poems on a particular day of the week, I was more likely to remember to include poetry in my shared reading experiences. Students would look forward to the poetry. Over time, I noticed that students would sometimes find a poem that they wanted me to share with the class. Poetry is helpful when teaching fluency and figurative language, processes and concepts that we can work on throughout the year.

Many teachers choose to focus on the *writing* of poetry in April because it is National Poetry Month. Provincial curriculum—with varying specificity—also indicates that students should experiment with writing poetry. Many teachers say that some of their typically more reluctant writers are motivated by the poetic form and the creativity involved in writing poetry. I too have found that I learn a lot about my students during this process. Writing poetry encourages students to play with language by manipulating words and the way they sound. If your curriculum is not specific as to which types students should try writing, consider these types: haiku, tanka, list poems, cinquain, limerick, sound poems, found poems, shape poems, acrostic poems, pantoum, and free verse. (Chapter 8 of *How Do I Get Them to Write?* explains and provides examples of each.)

The Writing Process at Work in Our Classrooms

If you are not a writer yourself, you may find the teaching of writing daunting. Many teachers do. When I give in-services on writing, I often ask teachers this question: *Do you assign written tasks to your students or do you teach your students how to write?* At the beginning of my career, I know I was assigning written tasks without truly teaching my students how to write. I now realize I was not empowering my students to become writers: I was not intentional about giving them the tools or confidence they needed. Perhaps some of it happened inadvertently, but I now look back knowing that my instruction could have been much more effective.

In *Freewriting with Purpose*, I included the following diagram to explain the process of teaching writing. That book goes into depth about each step into the process but I include a brief walkthrough here.

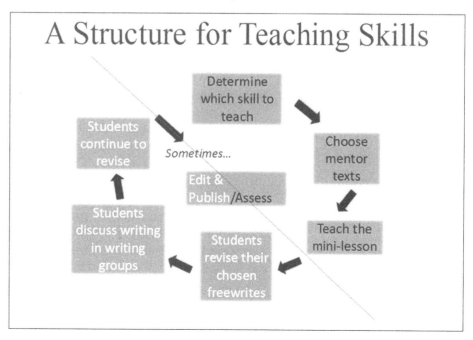

If you were to look back at the lesson on dialogue in Chapter 3, you will see how it follows this structure.

The process outlined in the diagram will be repeated in your classroom again and again. By following this structure, you will engage students in effective, meaningful learning. I have ensured that this practice capitalizes on the gradual release of responsibility. Notice that everything you see to the right of the line is what you as the teacher are doing; everything to the left of the line is what you will guide your students to do. On my weekly language arts schedule, I always ensure I have one longer language arts block that I dedicate to writing. This is the process I follow at that time.

Before we look at each step within the diagram, a point of clarification is needed. I've sometimes noticed the terms *revision* and *editing* being used interchangeably in classrooms despite being distinct processes. A helpful way to distinguish between the two is to think of our writing rubric. Revision typically deals with all of the elements of the rubric *except* conventions, those big decisions we make about our writing. Editing (for students) typically focuses on conventions, fine-tuning the details to make our work both readable and presentable.

Determine Which Skill to Teach

In their book *Clarity for Learning*, John Almarode and Kara Vandas (2019, 4) outline three essential questions that students should be able to answer during any given lesson:

1. What am I learning?
2. Why am I learning it?
3. How will I know I have learned it?

To begin, we must decide our learning intention. Which specific skill do we want to teach? I direct you to two main sources: your curricular outcomes (depending again how specific they are) and the writing rubric you use with students. When looking at a rubric, narrow your focus to one of the traits of writing and then look at the description under that trait. Think of each bullet point as a potential mini-lesson. Let's explore an example from both curriculum and a rubric.

One of the outcomes in the Grade 3 Alberta curriculum says, "Include a range of sentence beginnings and types to vary and add interest to writing." If we were to look at a writing rubric, this outcome would fall under sentence fluency. I would divide this outcome into two mini-lessons for my students. In fact, on most rubrics they are listed as two separate bullet points. The first mini-lesson would be on using "a range of sentence beginnings." As I'm sure you've noticed, a common feature of student writing in elementary school is the repetitive beginnings such as *Then... Then... Then* or *And... And... And*. A specific lesson in this area is time well spent. On another day, I would then teach "sentence types" which is the second half of that outcome. I typically connect a lesson on sentence types to punctuation. When we use a period at the end of a sentence, we create a *statement*. When we use a question mark at the end of a sentence, we create a *question*. When we use an exclamation mark, we create an *exclamation*. Student are more apt to remember to use punctuation when they are using it intentionally to create different sentence types. As the year goes on, we may also spend time exploring the difference between simple sentences, compound sentences, and complex sentences. From that one outcome—"Include a range of sentence beginnings and types to vary and add interest to writing"—we've just determined two or three potential mini-lessons that can build on each other from lesson to lesson. Whether you teach these in subsequent weeks or spread them out further will depend on your students. You can also look to connected outcomes or other bullet points in the sentence fluency column of the rubric for other ideas: sentence length being another topic for a mini-lesson.

You'll notice a very narrow focus to the mini-lessons. This is intentional. Students are much more likely to understand and apply the skill if we zero in on one area. Over time, students learn many techniques to make their writing more sophisticated.

Mentor Texts and Mini-Lessons

Whatever skill we are teaching, we need mentor texts to show exemplary writing. During our mini-lesson we will read and explore the mentor texts with students. Why? Ritchhart, Church, and Morrison (2011) explain it well:

> When we learn anything, we rely on models. We attend to what and how others are doing things, and we imitate them. This is as true and important for learning to learn and learning to think as it is for learning to dance or to play baseball. Imagine aspiring to be a great dancer without ever having seen great dancing. The novice imitates experts in an ever-advancing series of approximations of excellence, learning what works best for him- or herself along the way. (29)

If it becomes the norm in our classrooms, students at all grade levels understand how and why we use picture books as mentor texts.

If we want students to write sentences with a variety of sentence beginnings, we can explore quality literature so students can see what effective authors do. Most often, I read one entire mentor text aloud (a picture book is best for this purpose because of its length) and then analyze the craft of the writer in regard to that specific skill. Although writing with a variety of sentence beginnings seems obvious to us, many students have developed the habit of starting with the same word or group of words. *Telling* them to start with other words is certainly not as effective as *showing* them what other authors do. After a first mentor text, we explore excerpts from others. Capitalize on the interactive whiteboard for this purpose: showing a screenshot, putting the text under a document camera, using text from a digital library. Whatever works!

After I have shared examples with students, I release some of the responsibility onto my students and ask them to open a book and make observations about the writing specific to the skill I am teaching. *"Look at the sentence beginnings in the book you have. Does the author begin their sentences in all the same way? What are some of the first words or phrases you notice? Hands up and share your observations."* This step—which you also saw in the lesson on dialogue—is an important one before students look at their own writing.

Choose Freewrite and Begin Revising

Consider this: if your administrator walked in and asked any one of your students during your lesson *"What are you learning?"* and *"Why are you learning it?"*—could they answer? Structure your lesson so the answers are entirely clear to students.

After we have explored a number of mentor texts, I now ask students to look back at their own writing and make observations about their work. This was one of my big ah-ha moments when my students and I began freewriting regularly. Because they have a growing accumulation of writing, it is much more powerful for them to look back at something they've already written and notice their tendencies—rather than asking them to write something new. This significantly reduces the cognitive load during the lesson but it also makes them more reflective writers.

For most general writing skills—such as those on sentence fluency, adding detail, or word choice—our students' freewriting serves the purpose well. Students know they don't have to share *every* freewrite, but they understand they will be choosing some of their freewrites to use during mini-lessons throughout the year. Because they have choice, students are often excited to revisit their writing. When we are teaching skills more specific to a particular genre (such as dialogue within narrative writing or the use of text features in nonfiction text), we want students to look back at writing in that genre. If they've only written one narrative thus far, they must obviously use that narrative. This typically isn't a problem for students once they understand the purpose.

Have you ever asked your students to revise their writing and received blank stares in return? Many students don't know what we mean when we ask them to revise. Other students have the mindset that their writing is "done" the moment they finish writing it. A growth mindset is essential when working through the writing process. When I ask students to look back at their writing during my mini-lesson, at first, the goal is simply to have them make observations about their writing. Then, we take it one step further and guide them in revising their work based on the focus skill. I model this process as much as possible so they can see exactly what to do: in the example of a variety of sentence beginnings, they adjust their sentences to ensure they are varied.

Writing Groups

As we move through the diagram, you'll notice that students meet with their writing groups after the initial revision during the mini-lesson. What are writing groups? Think of them as critique groups: an opportunity to share writing with peers, giving and receiving feedback. Students are not actually writing during this time, but I have found this term has a more positive connotation for students as compared to critique groups.

I have encountered teachers who are hesitant about carving out time for writing groups. These same teachers are later astounded when they listen to their students giving meaningful feedback to one another. Understand, however, this meaningful dialogue does not just happen. It is essential to model the process and talk about the expected behaviors. The reason I include them immediately after the mini-lesson itself is because students are much more likely to use the language we were using to discuss the mentor texts. If you are still wary to make time for writing groups, in addition to outcomes on the writing process and revision, take a moment to consider the many curricular outcomes related to oral language, communication, collaboration, and critical thinking.

Have you ever watched *Austin's Butterfly*? This six-minute video by EL Education (Expeditionary Learning) convinces teachers and students of the power of feedback and the importance of multiple drafts. Before asking your students to work in writing groups, I encourage you to show this video—no matter the grade level—and discuss what they notice. Even though the video is about a scientific drawing and not writing, students absolutely see how our work can be improved when we are open to feedback.

I find pre-established groups of four most effective. Any larger and attention starts to wane as students share. Any smaller and students don't receive a lot of feedback. Because writing makes us vulnerable, and sharing our writing even more so, it is essential that students develop trust within their group. We model and practice respectful ways of providing feedback and remind students that the suggestions are not meant to be judgmental but rather helpful.

Revision after Writing Groups

After students receive feedback in their writing groups, it is important to give them time to continue revising, preferably immediately after they meet. To facilitate this, I ask the writing groups to meet somewhere other than their desks or tables. Then, as they finish with their groups, they return to their own places

It is imperative that our students understand that the feedback they give and receive is about the writing, the work, or the process, and not the individual.

Chapter 2 of *Freewriting with Purpose* includes a much more detailed explanation of how to establish and run writing groups in your classroom.

to revise independently. This accomplishes several things: it gives us a visual of which groups are still meeting, and we build in time for revision. We don't have to give them long—5 to 10 minutes is enough—but by providing this time, we encourage students to consider the feedback of their peers. If we simply move onto something else, students forget what their peers have said or just don't get around to revising based on the peer feedback.

By following this structure of teaching skills, and embedding revision into our mini-lessons, students learn how to revise their work. They are no longer confused by what we are asking them to do but often excited for the opportunity to make their writing stronger.

Editing

You'll notice in the centre of the diagram that students are not always asked to edit their work. Since they are writing often, there is no need to edit everything they write. In fact, if this is the expectation, editing becomes something they dread. My guideline—one that students are well-aware of—is that they are expected to edit anything they are handing in. This includes everything from journal entries to reports (in any subject area) to written answers on a test. My intention is to develop editing as a habit. I teach them to use the word wall, their phonemic knowledge, morphological awareness, and their sight-word vocabulary. They also look to see that the writing is punctuated properly. When we are intentional about asking them to edit what is being shared with others, they tend to see its value.

My favorite strategy for student editing is asking them to *read to the wall.* By reading out loud, without the distraction of others sitting nearby, they often catch errors they wouldn't otherwise. Pencil in hand, they fix any mistakes they notice. The first time through, they think it's odd; then, they begin asking to *read to the wall,* understanding its effectiveness!

The Importance of Feedback

To improve student writing, feedback is necessary. As a writer myself, it's hard to imagine not having the opportunity to receive feedback during my writing process; feedback from others pushes my thinking and ultimately improves my writing. Depending on their prior experiences, our students may not understand the importance of feedback. Once again, we must strive to develop a growth mindset and an environment where risk-taking is valued. When we do, they are open to the feedback of others—both teachers and peers—and their work will show significant improvement if we teach them how to revise based on the feedback they receive.

Keep in mind that "marking up" our students' writing and correcting their spelling, verb tense, grammar, or anything else is *not* feedback. This practice does nothing to improve our students' writing. In fact, the message perceived by students is often: *"Look at all of my mistakes. I'm not a good writer."* Students who receive this type of feedback rarely use the markings of the teacher to revise or edit their work and the emotional reaction is often strong. If you ever received this so-called feedback, you likely had a similar reaction. And really, if our ultimate goal for students is to transfer and apply their learning into their independent work, we shouldn't correct their mistakes *for* them. The other reason this "mark-up" is problematic is that we're pointing out *errors*. To me, feedback should be more than editing or correcting mistakes: effective feedback supports writers with both ideas and techniques, leading to revision.

Forms of Teacher Feedback

Feedback to students can be given in many forms: oral comments, written comments, references to a portion of the rubric, and the use of single-point rubrics. Keep in mind, for all forms of feedback, less is more!

Oral Feedback

During student writing time (except during freewriting when I am also writing), I engage in quick writing conferences with students. During the conference students share a portion of their writing and we simply talk. I can provide immediate feedback, differentiated for the student I am conferencing with. I try to meet with each student once a month to talk about their writing. As part of my planning, I put a sticky note on three students' desks the day before I intend to conference with them. This technique is effective for two reasons: first, it gives students time to think about what they want to share with me, and just as important, it holds me accountable. Within our hectic schedules, it may be tempting to skip the conferences because we are busy doing something else. But when students are expecting to meet, I will not disappoint them!

What occurs during this writing conference? To begin, students read me a portion of their writing that they've chosen ahead of time. Then, I let the students take the lead. They typically have questions about what they are sharing, often connected to a recent mini-lesson. If they don't have anything specific to discuss, I'll say, "*Tell me about your writing.*" This is usually enough to get them talking. I also add feedback based on what I noticed about their writing, and sometimes we set a goal together. These conferences do not take long: five to seven minutes is usually adequate. Through this one-on-one time, students feel valued as writers as we listen to their ideas, concerns, and questions.

Written Comments

Another way to provide feedback is through written comments. Our written comments might be given on sticky notes placed on students' writing or by using the comments feature in a digital format. I tend to avoid writing comments directly on my students' work. Some students might not mind this at all, while it may be intrusive for others. Remember, rather than "marking up" or commenting on many things, less is more. Target something you've been working on or one thing (not everything) that needs attention. Include a positive comment as well as feedback to help them improve.

Use a Portion of the Rubric

Just as we zero in on an area of the rubric for instruction, teaching one specific skill, we can do the same for feedback. If our most recent mini-lessons have been on word choice, we can isolate that column of the rubric and provide feedback to students on that particular skill. We might indicate what level of the rubric they are at and then add a short comment. This is intended as formative assessment, given to help students improve. Eventually, you might use the rubric as a summative assessment, but focusing on the formative piece will be the catalyst to improve student writing.

Single-Point Rubrics

Single-point rubrics have grown in popularity over the past few years: they provide opportunities to reflect on areas of improvement (GROW) and areas of strength (GLOW), and they tend to be user-friendly for students. I create the single-point rubrics based on the mini-lessons I teach. The focus of each mini-lesson becomes one of the criteria in the middle column. Staying with the word choice example, you can see how the language used in the criteria column can be adapted for your grade level and according to your specific lessons on the topic.

Single-point rubrics can be used for teacher feedback, peer feedback, and self-reflection.

Word Choice

GROW	CRITERIA for proficient performance/product	GLOW
	I can **find** interesting words used by an author.	
	I can **use specific** and **interesting** words in my writing.	
	I can **use descriptive words** to paint a picture in the reader's mind.	

Word Choice

GROW	CRITERIA for proficient performance/product	GLOW
	I can **find** interesting words used by an author.	
	I can use **specific nouns** and **adjectives** to add depth to my writing.	
	I can use lively **verbs** and appropriate **adverbs** to add energy to my writing.	
	I have used at least one form of **figurative language** (such as simile, metaphor, hyperbole) appropriately.	

Single-point rubrics can be created for any skill you are teaching. Some might be specific to narrative writing: dialogue, character development, setting, or any of the plot patterns, for example. Some might be specific to another form of text: text features, persuasive writing, opinion writing, or letter writing. You can also develop them for skills that apply to any genre of text: word choice, sentence fluency, punctuation, organization, or an effective beginning or ending. Notice though, you could adapt each of these to fit a particular genre. The organization of a narrative, for example, is certainly different from the organization of persuasive text or a nonfiction report.

Effective Feedback Should Be...

You will likely move from one form of feedback to another depending on the context. I use all of the forms explained in the previous pages throughout the year for different purposes. Regardless, there are certain qualities that make feedback especially effective: *timely*, *targeted*, and *actionable*.

Timely

Effective feedback is *timely*, given *throughout* the process of writing and not only at the completion of assignments. Feedback given at the end of a task is all too common in our classrooms. But if our goal is to strengthen their work, why not give students the opportunity to use the feedback in the current assignment? Also be careful that the feedback is timely in another way too: if weeks or months have passed before we give our feedback, there isn't much point. Students may have lost momentum or interest in the assignment.

Targeted

Our feedback to individual students should also be *targeted*, explaining both *what* and *how* they need to revise. By asking them to specifically look at the beginning of their story (or word choice, or the organization of their writing, or…), they know *what* we want them to focus on. By referring to one of our mini-lessons, we can support them with *how*.

When giving targeted feedback, it is most effective to include both positive and constructive feedback. As mentioned, single-point rubrics help guide this thinking: positive feedback (areas of GLOW) and constructive feedback (areas of GROW). When providing the positives, ensure your comments are specific to a particular technique or passage. If someone is reading a draft of my writing and says, *"Good work!"*, I don't know specifically what they liked: content, format, style? In contrast, if someone says, *"I like the way you…"*, I know exactly what is working, what they liked, and what I should keep. The same is true for our students. Constructive feedback also requires specific direction. After all, it is through constructive feedback that our students' writing will improve. If all comments are positive, there isn't reason to revise or push our thinking further.

Actionable

Our constructive comments lead to the third quality of effective feedback: *actionable*. After all, what's the point of giving or receiving feedback if nothing is done with it? What do we mean by actionable? Our comments will "equip the receiver to take action" (Almarode & Vandas 2019, 133). For example, if I have a student who wrote a page and a half of text without paragraphing, my feedback might be to remind them of our recent mini-lesson on organization and direct them to use the techniques we practiced together: first, I would encourage them to read their writing out loud, listening for natural topic breaks. I might also ask them to try to

"By being constructive, effective feedback serves a very useful purpose: learning" (Almarode & Vandas 2019, 136).

list the main topic and subtopics they included in their writing. These are actionable steps and provide them with an authentic opportunity to use the feedback. If I gave this feedback after the assignment was finished, they would not be able to improve their work and we've missed an opportunity for learning.

Sometimes, feedback directs students in what actions to take, and sometimes it targets an area but allows students to decide on their actions. Consider how your feedback might vary depending on the student or the time of year. Prompts such as *"Have you considered...?"* or *"I'm wondering if there is a way to..."* are still actionable, but again, we can release more responsibility onto our students. They must think critically and creatively to come up with a solution.

Writing Assessments

If you're leaving your classroom at the end of each and every week with a stack of student writing to assess, I'd encourage you to stop! Should we ever assess our students' writing? Certainly. But much of their writing—especially in elementary classrooms—should be low-stakes writing with no formal assessments attached. If you return to the diagram on page 119, you'll notice that in the centre, assessment is suggested *sometimes*. Most often, we will work through the outside of the diagram with the goal of improving student writing.

There are two unintended consequences of over-assessing our students' work: 1) students become (or remain) reluctant to write, and 2) teachers don't ask their students to write as much, believing it all has to be assessed.

The weekly forms of writing—journals, freewriting, and reader response—are rarely, if ever, assessed. Perhaps we assess one of our students' freewriting or reader response on occasion, but only if students have had an opportunity to prepare by revising and editing before the assessment. It is the other forms of writing, those that are spread throughout the year, that we will assess—most often, through rubrics.

Rubrics

The benefit of assessing through rubrics is the breakdown into the various elements of writing. The 6 + 1 Traits of Writing (ideas and content, organization, voice, word choice, sentence fluency, and conventions, with presentation being the +1) were introduced by Ruth Culham and are the most common in elementary classrooms. The rubrics based on these traits can be used and adapted for many genres of writing.

Remember, rubrics are not only used for assessment, they are helpful throughout the process of teaching writing. Think back to the questions posed by Almarode and Vandas: *What am I learning? Why am I learning it? How will I know I have learned it?* Rubrics can be used to determine your learning intentions, and then shared with students. They can also be used for feedback.

If you have grade colleagues, I highly recommend using the same rubric and periodically assessing your students' writing collaboratively to ensure your standards are similar.

Although the teaching of writing is complex, thinking through your approach and planning carefully will empower you to instill confidence and build competence in your student writers.

8

Literacy in the Content Areas

"Reading is the gateway skill that makes all other learning possible."
— Barack Obama

The Power of Integration: Authenticity

In elementary schools, teachers are responsible for teaching most subjects to their students. This structure provides incredible opportunities. By entrenching literacy skills and strategies into all subject areas, our students benefit immensely. Some may argue that literacy skills are present in the other subjects whether we are intentional or not. This is true. However, I'm referring to making the integration between subject areas both deliberate and transparent for students.

"Do the best you can until you know better. Then when you know better, do better." — Maya Angelou

I have a confession to make: as an elementary teacher, I did not capitalize on the power of integration as much as I now realize I should have. I missed golden opportunities to help students understand content curriculum *and* enhance their literacy skills. I regret that I didn't bring science text to my guided reading groups. I regret that it took many years of teaching before I realized the power of having students write to construct meaning in all areas of the curriculum. I regret the rigidity of my elementary timetable, not realizing how the intentional integration of subjects could enhance my instruction and ultimately improve student learning.

Fast forward to today: I now present sessions about leveraging literacy strategies to improve understanding across the curriculum. These sessions are applicable not only in elementary classrooms but at all levels. It is rewarding to see junior high math teachers or high school biology teachers recognize the power of bringing literacy strategies into their classrooms with more intention. The advantage at the elementary level is that we're teaching most subjects to our students. We can immediately apply the literacy strategies or skills we've taught that very day or week into other areas of our curriculum. Often, our administrators ask us to submit a timetable where we separate the subjects to ensure we allocate enough minutes for each. Even when doing so, I encourage you to see beyond the silos of the subjects you teach to ensure literacy is leveraged beyond the language arts classroom.

The Importance of Background Knowledge

Have you ever given a reading assessment to a student and been surprised at the results? Consider the student who decodes well but has limited comprehension of the text. These results often point to a lack of background knowledge connected to the text. Willingham (2017) concurs:

> We might think that reading tests provide an all-purpose measure of reading ability. But we've seen that reading comprehension depends heavily on how much the reader happens to know about the topic of the text. Perhaps then, reading comprehension tests are really knowledge tests in disguise. (127)

At times, our students seem to be proficient readers with fiction text, but with nonfiction text, especially text in other subject areas, proves difficult. If students do not have background knowledge in an area, or are not familiar with the vocabulary, their understanding of the content or concept will be limited. If we return to the Simple View of Reading, this makes sense.

Word Recognition × Language Comprehension = Reading Comprehension

Language comprehension includes both vocabulary and background knowledge. We can use all the strategies we've got, but without background knowledge about a topic, our comprehension may still be limited. In their book *Subjects Matter*, Harvey Daniels and Steven Zemelman (2014) provide this example of text:

> The Batsmen were merciless against the Bowlers. The Bowlers placed their men in slips and covers. But to no avail. The Batsmen hit one four after another along with an occasional six. Not once did their balls hit their stumps or get caught. (27)

The first time I read this paragraph (and instinctively reread it to see if I could make more sense of it), my comprehension was limited. I am able to decode all of the words, and in fact, I understand most of the individual words, but still, the paragraph didn't make a lot of sense to me. Was your experience similar? Does your understanding change when you're told this passage is about the game of cricket? It did for me! Reading it again—knowing the topic—I understood more than I did at first. But because I haven't played or watched the game, there were still gaps in my comprehension. Perhaps the same is true for you.

Through this example, the role of background knowledge in comprehension becomes clear. Imagine those students who read about blizzards and ice fishing and tobogganing without ever having experienced winter! Imagine our students who are reading about the states of matter for the first time. Their experiences connected to a topic—or lack thereof—will influence their comprehension. Some students may make connections to their ice cream melting or the steam from a tea kettle. Others may not. The more we can support the connections to their background knowledge and involve them in such discussions, the better. In *The Knowledge Gap*, Natalie Wexler cites a research example that demonstrates the importance of prior knowledge. In the study, a group of preschool children were read a book about birds; researchers had established that the children in the higher-income bracket knew more about the topic prior to the read-aloud. Afterwards, all children were tested on their comprehension. As expected, those

Background knowledge plays a role in many of the strategies we ask our students to use: *making predictions, making connections, inferring,* and even *asking questions* to some degree.

with background knowledge about the topic demonstrated significantly better comprehension. Researchers then read a story about an invented animal called wugs: "When prior knowledge was equalized, comprehension was essentially the same. In other words, the gap in comprehension wasn't a gap in skills. It was a gap in knowledge" (Wexler 2019, 30).

Willingham suggests,

> Teaching reading is not just a matter of teaching reading. The whole curriculum matters, because good readers have broad knowledge in civics, drama, history, geography, science, the visual arts, and so on. (127)

When we integrate literacy into the content areas, we are able to support our students in significant ways. This integration should not be seen as an add-on when it's convenient but as a powerful, evidence-based practice occurring on a daily basis.

Enhancing Reading Comprehension Across the Curriculum

To support students with nonfiction texts across various subject matters, we can leverage the instructional practices we discussed in Chapter 6—read-alouds, shared reading, guided reading, partner reading, and independent reading—to improve understanding in all areas of the curriculum.

Read-Alouds

Be transparent about applying reading strategies throughout the day, every day.

You likely read aloud in various subject areas already—whether it be a picture book or an excerpt of text. But do you use these opportunities to reinforce literacy strategies as you do in language arts? For example, while reading text aloud in science, we can be intentional about thinking aloud when decoding morphologically complex words, breaking down the word into its morphemes. We can review the meaning of the morphemes and discuss them in relation to the text. Or, if we had been talking about the strategy of visualization earlier in the week, we can use this strategy as we discuss a historical context in social studies. These strategies become grounded in authentic practice as students use them throughout the curriculum.

The reading aloud of content-area text is actually quite important. Often, the nonfiction text within the content-area curriculum has unfamiliar vocabulary and the content may require us to draw upon prior knowledge. By reading the text to students instead of asking them to read it independently, we can support them with comprehension through timely discussion about both the vocabulary and the content. We also model strategies in action, such as rereading text a second time through. Some students believe that this is something "poor" readers do. I want them to experience how the rereading of text can improve our understanding and it is actually a strategy that "good" readers use.

Shared Reading

In addition to reading aloud content-area text, consider the opportunities for shared reading. As we discussed in Chapter 6, round-robin reading is not an

Make the learning process as transparent as possible for your students.

effective practice and yet is often used when teachers want to share text in various curricular areas. Instead, consider how shared reading can support student understanding. Begin by reading a paragraph of text that students all have access to, such as something in a textbook or something displayed digitally. After you've read this paragraph *to* them, ask students to read it *with* you. There is no need to put one student on the spot. Through shared reading, we can better engage all students and support their understanding through timely, responsive conversations about vocabulary and content. You can also guide them to make predictions and connections, which both depend on students activating their prior knowledge. Should we talk only about the vocabulary and the content? Certainly not. These are prime opportunities to discuss how we learn and how we use particular strategies when we read. We might even talk about Rosenblatt's Reader Response Theory (see page 115) and how it applies while reading nonfiction text.

Guided Reading

Bring text from your content-area curriculum to your guided reading table. Consider: Which students would benefit from reading this text with you in a small-group setting before you tackle it as a class? What is the focus during this time: vocabulary, content, reading strategies? Willingham suggests bringing it all together. By the time we get to our social studies or science lesson, we have empowered those who would typically struggle with the content by previewing and discussing it during guided reading. We can also reinforce specific strategies needed by that particular group of students.

Partner Reading

Students should be given opportunities to read and discuss text in partners across the curriculum and at all grade levels. They can support each other with both reading the text and making meaning from the content. Encourage them to alternate reading the paragraphs or sections of text, and guide them to discuss the content briefly after each section. Remind them to use the strategies you have been teaching—predicting, connecting, summarizing, visualizing, etc.—and to clarify their understanding of both vocabulary and content. Reading and discussing text with a partner is a form of accountability. After students get used to this instructional practice occurring in various subject areas, discuss the process together. *"How does reading with a partner help you understand the content? Do you like this practice? Why or why not?"*

Other Scaffolds to Improve Comprehension

Since previous chapters talked at length about turn-and-talk opportunities (or Think-Pair-Share), I didn't include this strategy here. However, it is an indispensable strategy, useful for enhancing student comprehension throughout the day and in all subject areas.

In addition to thinking about background knowledge and instructional contexts for reading, there are other language scaffolds, cooperative learning strategies, and thinking routines that we can use to help improve comprehension and learning in all areas of the curriculum.

Frontloading with Images

In Chapter 4, we talked about using images to develop students' questioning skills. In *Subjects Matter*, Daniels and Zemelman explain another purpose for images. Before reading a passage or beginning a new unit of study, we can project images to frontload information for students. You may choose to show only part

Are you about to start a new unit in social studies? Consider showing images of artifacts, or of specific locations or buildings, to get students talking about the upcoming topic of study.

of one image and discuss that portion before revealing another part and adding to the discussion. (This strategy of looking at a small portion of an image first is sometimes referred to as Zoom In or Crop It!) Eventually students will see and discuss the whole image. You might decide instead to show a group or series of images. Depending on the topic, you could reveal one image at a time or show the images all at once. Begin by asking students to make observations about the images and then to articulate what they notice or what they are thinking about to a partner. By discussing the image, or series of images, students will begin to understand such things as the content, context, problem, or people that may be involved in what they are about to read or study. As you bring your discussion to the whole group, students may build on one another's thoughts. Considering how prevalent images are in today's society, this is an effective way to capture our students' attention and teach them how to *read* visual images. It some ways, it also levels the playing field as it does not require students to read printed text in order to understand. "Then, once we have built background knowledge and evoked curiosity, we can make a better transition to printed material" (Daniels & Zemelman 2014, 100).

Reciprocal Teaching

You may choose to reinforce reciprocal teaching during a guided reading session. This enables you to provide support to students as they experience the process.

This cooperative learning strategy was first introduced in the 1980s by Annemarie Sullivan Palincsar and Ann L. Brown. Reciprocal teaching focuses on four strategies: predicting, clarifying, questioning, and summarizing. Although the model has been modified in many ways since its creation, typically, students work in groups of four and use the four strategies to monitor their understanding before, during, and after reading. In elementary classrooms, it tends to be most effective when we assign one strategy to each student in the group and they take on a teaching role for that strategy. As they read the text, students stop periodically to monitor their understanding using one of the four strategies. Depending on the age of your students, their familiarity with the reading strategies, or their previous experience with reciprocal teaching, it may be worth practicing each strategy as a whole class first and scaffolding the experience by providing specific prompts. Creating an anchor chart with the four strategies and some appropriate sentence starters will also support students when they begin with their groups.

Fisher, Frey, and Hattie (2016) explain the effectiveness of this strategy: "researchers have found it to be effective with students with disabilities, English learners, and bilingual students" (98). The ultimate goal: students begin to use the strategies independently after practicing them in a scaffolded setting with peer support.

Conversation Round Tables

A few years ago, I attended a session with Doug Fisher and Nancy Frey where they led participants through a conversation round table. The goal of this strategy is to help students more fully understand the content they are reading about. Students work in groups of four and are given a passage of text—an article, a textbook page, whatever is appropriate in your context. They begin by reading the passage independently and writing jot notes about the content in the top left corner of a graphic organizer (similar to the one following).

Title of text:		Name:
1. My notes		2. What _____ said
	My independent summary	
3. What _____ said		4. What _____ said

Remember, another strategy that can support comprehension is representing: "Use pictures and words to demonstrate your understanding" (see page 27). You might use this strategy independently or combine it with another thinking routine or framework, such as a conversation round table.

After students have made their individual notes, each person shares their ideas about the text with the group. The other group members jot down the ideas in the corresponding box. Once everyone has shared, students write a short summary of the text in the centre, considering their own initial understanding and also the ideas of their peers. During this process it becomes clear that we interpret text somewhat differently and that our own understandings may change as we listen to our peers.

Connect-Extend-Challenge

The Connect-Extend-Challenge thinking routine reminds me of a KWL Chart (what I *Know*, what I *Want* to know, what I *Learned*) that many teachers use with students. I prefer the terminology in Connect-Extend-Challenge as it is more aligned with how we discuss the process of learning with students. In the first column—Connect—ask students to describe how the ideas they read or heard about *connect* with what they already know. Explain how this refers to their background knowledge about a topic. In the second column—Extend—ask students to write down the new information they have learned, information that is now *extending* their knowledge. In the third column—Challenge—ask students to reflect on *challenges*, questions, or confusions they might have after learning the new information.

Consider providing a simple graphic organizer to students the first few times they are completing this framework. As they become familiar with the process, they can easily create one in their notebooks.

Connect *Information I already know*	Extend *New information learned*	Challenge *Questions I have*

Consider the many situations where this framework might be effective: after watching a video in science class, after a shared reading experience in social studies, after a field trip or guest speaker, or even after learning a technique in art class. The possibilities are endless!

After using this framework in the classroom, I have witnessed some students initiate using it independently in other contexts: a surefire sign that it is effective.

Annotating Text

If you were to look through most of my resources, you would find notes or questions in the margins, underlined text, and often sticky notes to flag particular sections or pages. Why? Annotating text in this way helps me slow down, react, and process what I am reading. When I return to a particular text, it is also useful to see my reactions and connections right on the pages themselves. Students benefit from annotating text as well. The problem elementary teachers encounter is that most of the text shared in the classroom is used by students from year to year. If you are lucky enough to have a set of texts that belong to your current students, take the opportunity to teach them to annotate.

Once again, consider how an anchor chart might be helpful to students as they are learning to annotate text.

Even though there is really no right or wrong way to annotate, students will need to see you model annotation before they know what to do on their own. Project an article, test, or other text so it is visible to all students. Then, annotate the text as you read aloud and think-aloud. Make your thinking visible to students so they know why you are annotating the way you are. You may want to present categories to students so they know the kinds of annotations they could make: important points, connections, questions, clarifications (about content or vocabulary), and even confusions are important to note. In addition to comments, you might also encourage students to use symbols: a happy face or check mark indicating something they agree with, a question mark indicating a confusion, a star or asterisk for something that they think is important, and an exclamation mark for something surprising. Remind students that there isn't one right way and encourage them to develop a system that works for them.

After you have modelled this process a few times, give all students an excerpt of text in printed form and ask them to annotate the page. (Copyright allows us to copy up to 10% of a text. Photocopying or printing one page of a science textbook for students to practice annotation is certainly within this parameter.) After students annotate a page individually, ask them to meet with a partner to discuss their annotations: what was similar or different? Then, bring this discussion to the whole class. The same process can be followed for annotating test questions. We can model the highlighting or underlining of key words in the questions and also show the process of elimination of answers in a multiple-choice question. Annotating is an effective strategy for students on the tests we give in science, social studies, or math to ensure they take the time to understand what is being asked.

Enhancing Vocabulary Development Across the Curriculum

Have you ever tried to read a medical textbook with many unfamiliar words? If we don't understand much of the vocabulary and have to look up word after word after word, our comprehension will be limited and we probably won't persist for very long. This may be the experience for some of our students with content-area text. Vocabulary development *is* essential for our student readers. As Wexler (2019) points out, "kids with less overall knowledge and vocabulary are always at a disadvantage" (31). I've noticed that struggles with text seem to become more apparent in upper elementary. Wexler (2019) concurs: "Often, the difficulties begin to emerge in fourth grade, when children are confronted with nonfiction and texts that use more sophisticated vocabulary" (31). Knowing the importance of vocabulary, we would be remiss if we didn't work to develop our students' vocabulary. Some of our vocabulary instruction may occur during language arts, but often this instruction is most effective as we encounter the vocabulary in whatever subject we happen to be teaching.

In Chapter 5, we outlined the Three Tiers of Vocabulary. A focus on Tier Two words (academic words that cross disciplinary boundaries) and Tier Three words (content-specific words) are both essential for comprehension. As teachers, we are typically better at supporting students with Tier Three vocabulary since we expect that many of the words will be new to students. On the other hand, our teaching of Tier Two vocabulary is not always as explicit. Regardless of which tier we are referring to, Fisher, Frey, and Hattie (2016) remind us that "Learning a word requires not just exposure, but also repetition, contextualization, and authentic reasons to use the terminology in discussion, reading, and writing" (50). A one-time reference to a new word is not enough. The activities and strategies suggested in this section—in addition to reading the words in multiple contexts—will help students engage, manipulate, and utilize the words in various ways with the goal of internalizing the words and transferring their understanding in many contexts.

Vocabulary Preview

Before beginning a new unit, give students the topic or the name of the unit and have them predict the vocabulary words they might encounter. For example, if they are going to be studying animal life cycles in science, or government and responsible citizenship in social studies, ask them to work with a small group or partner to generate a list of words they expect to come across during this unit of study. Essentially, this task will begin to activate their prior knowledge. After they have a list of words, share a few of the key vocabulary words from the unit with them to see if they had the words on their list. If not, encourage them to add them. Ask students to pick three words from their list and write a predicted definition for each. Once they are familiar with morphology, writing predicted definitions tends to be easier and, in fact, students become quite excited to find the morphemes within the words to help them predict meaning with more accuracy.

Word Sorts

You may need to differentiate your word sorts for some students. You could provide the intended headings of the columns or have students work in partners so they can talk through their thinking. Some students may benefit from having the words on cards with an accompanying picture.

Word sorts are a simple yet powerful strategy to get students thinking more deeply about the meaning of words, their connections to each other, and the related concepts. They can be used in any subject area and at various points in your teaching. I especially like using them as review to gauge student understanding.

Let's look at a few examples. In math, I might give my students the following words: *gram, hour, kilometre, metre, second, milligram, kilogram, centimetre, millimetre, minute, tonne, day*. All of these words relate to measurement. I ask students to sort the words into three columns and create a heading for each.

I created this list based on three categories: measurement of *time*, *weight*, and *distance*.

measuring time	measuring weight	measuring distance
hour	gram	kilometre
second	milligram	metre
minute	kilogram	centimetre
day	tonne	millimetre

This is the way I anticipate my students will sort the words, however, I keep the word sort purposefully open-ended because it encourages them to think critically and creatively in terms of categories. After students have sorted the words on their own, I ask them to pair up and articulate why they sorted the words in the way they did. Perhaps they have a plausible explanation or categories other than the ones we intended.

Consider this word list example for science, again with the intent of three categories: *air, seedling, stem, sunlight, seed, water, leaves, nutrients, sprout, flowers, roots, plant*. I chose the words to fit into these categories: *parts of a plant, plant requirements for growth*, and *the life cycle of a plant*. After some exploration and thought, students will often recognize the concepts or categories from our recent teaching and organize the words in the same way we intended. Again, I would ensure I give them time to articulate their thinking to a partner after sorting the words. I use this time to circulate and listen to their explanations. A student might choose to sort the words according to the number of syllables in each. Is this wrong? Not if we have left the sort open-ended. In this case, after applauding the student's attention to the structure of words, I might challenge them to now sort the words according to content.

Is a word sort an effective use of time in math or science? Absolutely! Still unsure? Try one and listen to the quality of discussion about words, their meaning, and the connected concepts. Word sorts provide an opportunity to deepen a students' understanding in any area of the curriculum.

Concept Circles

With any of these strategies, be sure to capitalize on the role of oral language in learning by having students talk through their ideas and articulate their thinking with their peers.

Another simple yet effective strategy is the use of a concept circle. Begin by dividing a circle into four parts with a smaller circle in the centre. Fill in three parts of the larger circle with three connected words or phrases. For example, in social studies, I might write: *protest, elections*, and *freedom*. The fourth section of the large circle and the smaller circle in the middle are left blank. Students are asked to think about the connection between the three words and determine the overall concept (in this case, *democracy*) which they would write in the centre. Then, they determine a fourth word that connects to the other words under the concept of *democracy*: for example, *equality, representation, rule by the people*, or *freedom of the press*.

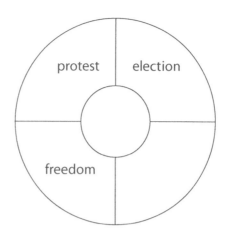

Although this example is designed for older students, we can also apply the same concept for younger learners. I might provide these three words connected to science: *lake, pond,* and *wetlands.* If we're at the end of a unit, students would likely recognize that these are all *bodies of freshwater* and write that phrase in the small circle in the centre. They would also choose another word to write in the fourth space of the large circle: *stream, river,* or *bog,* for example. To support younger students as they learn this strategy, be sure to model an example.

The possibilities for concept circles are endless, and yet they are a quick way of getting students to use, and think about, the vocabulary they are learning.

Generative Sentences

Have you ever asked students to write sentences with the vocabulary words you are teaching? Many teachers do, with good intentions: they want students to show their understanding of words by using them appropriately in a sentence. Unfortunately, I have witnessed students who give the same sentence for each word, just replacing the word itself, ultimately defeating the purpose of the task. The sentences may make sense but they certainly do not demonstrate an understanding of the meaning of the words. What's more: many students find this task rather dull. By adding certain constraints, we make the activity more motivating for our students.

Creating generative sentences—another strategy introduced to me by Fisher and Frey—has become a favorite vocabulary activity in many classrooms. For this activity, students are given certain parameters to follow when writing their sentences: the position of the word in the sentence and the length of the sentence. Here are a few examples with science vocabulary:

I give a limited number of words because writing these sentences requires some time and thought. Another example of less is more.

Word	Position	Length of Sentence
magnet	2nd	< eight words
force	3rd	= seven words
attract	4th	> five words

Word	Position	Length of Sentence
habitat	3rd	> five words
mammal	6th	= six words
adapt	5th	< ten words
survival	2nd	< seven words

One important note: students cannot change the form of the word you give by adding or removing a suffix, for example. The word must stay in its given form. When creating your table, play around with the words to ensure that what you are asking is plausible.

Watching a group of students (or adults) complete this activity is fascinating. It's like you can both see and hear the thinking going on in the room. Students tend to like this activity because they see it as a challenge. You'll hear them counting the words in a sentence and trying to adjust a sentence to make it work: sometimes adding an adjective to change the position of the word, or trying to rephrase or restructure the sentence entirely. Teachers like this activity because students are inevitably thinking about the meaning and context of the words, and they often use other vocabulary words from the unit in their sentences as well! If you want to capitalize on the language arts connections further, discuss the part of speech of each word before you begin.

Look at the first vocabulary word: habitat. *What part of speech is the word* habitat? *You're right, it's a noun. What position do we need this word in a sentence? Third. Okay, so I couldn't begin my sentence with 'The* habitat....' *What would I need to do to make it the third word in the sentence? You're right. I could be more specific. We could start with something like 'The rainforest habitat...' or 'The beaver's habitat....'*

By talking through an example, students will be better equipped to play with language and make the adjustments on their own.

Word Continuums

Some provincial curricular documents include vocabulary outcomes that refer to words (and their meanings) in relation to each other or to words on a scale. Word continuums target these outcomes explicitly.

Word continuums are sometimes referred to as semantic gradients. The idea is that a group of related words are placed on a continuum. For example, you might ask students to generate a long list of words that refer to temperature: *hot, cold, warm, boiling, sweltering, cool, freezing, brisk, chilly, nippy, mild, scorching,* etc. After the class has created this list, provide students with cards or slips of paper where they will write each word. Then, with a partner, students put the words along a continuum according to meaning: moving the words around as they discuss their meanings in relation to each other. For this example, it can be effective to write or place the words along the visual of a thermometer. If students decide *freezing* is the word on the list that implies the coldest temperature, it would go at the bottom of the thermometer. If they decide that *boiling* implies the hottest temperature, they would place it at the top of the thermometer. They would then place the other words in between, all relative to the each other. I have heard some fantastic debates about words and their meaning during this activity: students trying to justify why they think *scorching* should be above *boiling,* for instance.

You may have noticed that the words in each list are the same part of speech. In the examples referring to temperature and size, the words are all adjectives. In the examples referring to the way someone speaks and moves, the words are all verbs. Encourage students to stay consistent when listing the words as this creates a perfect opportunity to review parts of speech.

Other examples? Think about words describing size: *small, large, big, enormous, humongous, tiny, minuscule, gigantic, little, teensy, huge*. Words describing the volume at which someone speaks: *talk, shout, yell, whisper, exclaim, mutter, murmur, bellow*. Or words to describe the speed at which someone moves: *run, walk, jog, sprint, meander, wander, crawl, race, stroll, saunter*. As you can see, even the first task of generating a list of words exposes students to new words and draws attention to the idea of synonyms and antonyms. So, while the words may be science-related, you can reinforce or teach the related language arts outcomes too.

This activity is especially effective for explaining *connotation*, which can sometimes be a difficult concept for students to understand. By exploring the list of words they create, you might talk about which words have positive, or perhaps negative, connotations. Some words would be considered neutral: the word *talk* for example doesn't have either a positive or negative connotation. However, ask students about the word *mumble* or *chat*? How do they interpret these words, positively or negatively?

Morphology

We can't possibly teach our students every word they need to know. Thankfully, by teaching morphology, we can equip students with an understanding of words and their parts (morphemes) to help them figure out the meaning of many words. As you recall from Chapter 5, we teach morphology to our students within language arts but there are many cross-curricular connections. Look at these words, common in elementary classrooms: *centimetre, prediction, thermometer, herbivore, symphony, community, geography*. These words all contain morphemes that can be explicitly taught to students. Although we could teach them during language arts, it is more effective to teach them when they turn up in context during math, science, music, or social studies. Spending time in math discussing the meaning of numeric prefixes will help students with your current content but also support them when they encounter the morphemes in other words too.

I was presenting to a group of teachers and asked them to think of words with the root *phon* (sometimes spelled *phone*). As predicted they came up with words such as *phonics, phoneme, phonological, telephone, microphone, megaphone, phonograph, symphony, xylophone*, and more. I was explaining that words with the same morpheme are related through both structure (spelling) and meaning. Since the Greek root *phon* means "sound," then the meaning of the words with this root will all be connected to that meaning. For example, the word *telephone* includes the prefix *tele-* meaning "at a distance" and the root *phon* meaning "sound"; *telephone* literally means "sound at a distance." As I finished this explanation, a teacher in the audience exclaimed: *"Megaphone! BIG sound. I get it!"* Good ol' morphology. Students will begin to see these same connections as this teacher did in that moment.

Consider a science lesson on thermal energy. A teacher familiar with morphemes could talk about the word *thermal* and highlight the root *therm* for students. Just as I had teachers do with the root *phon*, students could generate a list of words that use the root *therm*: *thermometer, thermos, thermostat, hypothermia*, for example. Rather than telling students the meaning of the root, I prefer to give them the opportunity to turn-and-talk to see if they can determine the meaning based on what they know about the words. Many students will be able to come up with the actual meaning, or something related. Moving forward, then, they know that when they encounter a word with the morpheme *therm*, it has something to do with "heat."

When students are morphologically aware, they will begin to recognize word parts (which helps them with both decoding and encoding) and they will also be able to figure out the meaning of words in all areas of the curriculum.

In *Bug Club Morphology*, one of the suggestions I give to teachers is to create a small bulletin board called Word Wonderings. When students come across a word they are wondering about, they add it to the bulletin board. These words could be ones that students investigate during free time or ones that you explore as a class. Once they have a beginning understanding of morphology, they become quite excited to figure out new words. This opportunity for ongoing word investigations generates curiosity and excitement surrounding words.

Writing to Learn Across the Curriculum

We can learn a lot from our students. When I first introduced freewriting to my class, I used it in language arts. It hadn't yet occurred to me that it would be an effective process in other subject areas as well. Then, one day, a student asked, *"Can we freewrite about this?"* in a subject other than language arts. *"Why yes, yes we can."* And from that day forward I now incorporate writing into all areas of the curriculum. When we do, our students will be *writing to learn*: a way of thinking on the page, constructing meaning as they write. Although I was aware of this function of writing for myself—in fact, I use it often—it was yet another student who reinforced this function for students in the classroom. After we had finished freewriting and were quietly reading our writing to ourselves, one of my students exclaimed, *"I didn't know I thought that!"* My reaction and that of the class was to laugh, not at him, but at the truth to his words and the moment itself. I thanked him for his exclamation and we talked about writing as thinking on the page. The quote at the beginning of Chapter 7 by Isaac Asimov confirms this function: "Writing, to me, is simply thinking through my fingers." And Barack Obama once said,

> Writing has been an important exercise to clarify what I believe, what I see, what I care about, what my deepest values are. The process of converting a jumble of thoughts into coherent sentences makes you ask tougher questions.

Consider how effective freewriting might be after a science experiment or field trip, after watching a news clip or video in social studies, or after a quiet walk in nature. Freewriting in the content areas provides students with the opportunity to construct meaning, process what they've learned, and figure out how it connects to what they already know. Once again, this low-stakes writing—writing that will not be assessed and shared only if students choose—is powerful. When I invite students to share all or some of their freewrite in these other subject areas, their writing gives me insight into their understanding and thought processes. Their personal connections may also lead us to discuss related topics, themes, or issues.

Since freewriting works best when our elementary students use a prompt, I often provide options when writing across the curriculum. For example, after watching a science demonstration, I might put three prompts on the board: *I noticed...*, *I think...*, and *I wonder....* Students can move in and out of the prompts as they connect with them. Sometimes, to explore what they've learned, I might ask them to use two prompts: *I used to think...* and *But now I know....* This is especially effective at the end of a unit.

There are many situations when our students can be *writing to learn*. If you begin to use this process regularly, and talk about why, students will understand that this writing will not be assessed but that it is a way for them to think through the page.

Digital Literacy

There's no avoiding technology these days. It has become fundamental to all we do. Once when I was a consultant, the tech was "down"—no access to email, or Google slides or documents. I felt lost. It made me realize how dependent I had become on these tools. Our students—and even some of you, as teachers—have not experienced a world where we are not connected to devices.

Technology has changed our habits and the ways we read and write, and not all of these changes are positive. There seems to be an ever-present need for stimulation, a need to multitask. Many teachers suggest their students' ability to focus on sustained tasks has become challenging. Even if we accept and embrace technology, we still want students to be able to slow down their thinking and interact with the printed page. In *Reader, Come Home: The Reading Brain in a Digital World*, Maryanne Wolf (2018) suggests,

> The most important contribution of the invention of written language to the species is a democratic foundation for critical, inferential reasoning and reflective capacities. This is the basis of a collective conscience. If we in the twenty-first century are to preserve a vital collective conscience, we must ensure that all members of our society are able to read and think both deeply and well. We will fail as a society if we do not educate our children and reeducate all of our citizenry to the responsibility of each citizen to process information vigilantly, critically, and wisely across media. (200–201)

Within our classrooms, then, we must find a way to balance our students' interactions with the printed page and also teach them how to navigate the digital world. I have been in classrooms that teachers have declared as "paperless." Although well-intentioned, the reality is we shouldn't use one form of text at the exclusion of the other. Our students should become comfortable and proficient reading all forms.

Interacting with Digital Text

How do you define *text*? How does your curriculum define it? The definition expands each time a new platform is introduced. The traditional forms of text still exist, but we must also consider other types of text students encounter on a daily basis.

In elementary school, one of the curricular goals is the ability to research. In today's world, I can't imagine *not* using the internet to find information. And yet, with the onset of the internet also came the ability for anyone to publish anything. Fisher, Frey, and Hattie (2016) explain how this affects our students:

The Internet is an excellent source for digital material, but it is fraught with problems that can derail student projects. Chief among them are issues of credibility and accuracy of information. (96)

Our students must be taught to read carefully and consider the source of the information they receive. Studies have shown how easily students (and adults) are fooled by information shared online. The pervasiveness of fake news and inaccurate information is staggering. It is essential to consider our goals when using digital text. If we want students to find information to write a report, for example, we can find credible sources and websites ahead of time for them to reference. If our goal is to help them critically evaluate websites and information, we can explore and analyze sites and text together. With support, they can become more discerning readers of digital text; this is not something we want them to navigate alone.

We should also model how to put the information they have found through research into their own words. This is an exceptionally challenging task for most students and modelling—not once, but many times—will help students learn to do this on their own.

Writing on a Device

It is also important our students write *in class* rather than at home for homework so we know what they are capable of independently, especially with the increasing prevalence of generative AI.

I am typing as I write. I couldn't imagine writing an entire book by hand. I would miss the many tools embedded within the technology. And yet, for elementary-aged students in particular, writing on a computer or other device is not typically best practice. Most of the writing they do should be on paper. Remember, they are beginning writers. Think of all the skills they have to apply when writing: the physical act of forming of letters, phonetic and morphological awareness, the structure of a sentence, not to mention the meaning they want to convey. When we add technology to the mix, we are adding a whole new skillset: finding the letters on a keyboard and typing. Most elementary-aged students are not proficient at typing and this becomes a hindrance as they try to generate and record their thoughts. Typing one letter at a time does not lead to fluent writing. Journal writing, freewriting, and reader response are all ideal opportunities to print or handwrite. We want our students to explore emotional connections and relay experiences: the relationship between a writer and the pen or pencil as writing tool lends itself to this type of thinking on the page. I usually have students write initial drafts of narratives or transactional writing on paper, too. It is during the initial drafts where content is being generated. If you are asking older students to revise and publish a particular piece of writing, you might bring technology into the mix at this time. In fact, typing their report could be their typing practice. They've already written it so we're not interfering with the creation of content. Then, once they have a typed version, we can teach them the tools that make revision so convenient: inserting, reorganizing, or deleting text with ease, for example.

One other note about digital writing: some students become so accustomed to using textese outside of our classrooms that this shorthand finds its way into their classroom writing. By discussing the various text forms and structures, we can talk about the etiquette and appropriate conventions of each. It is appropriate to include shorthand and use limited punctuation in a text message; in a report, not so much. Have fun with these comparisons and use this conversation to your advantage to spark some fun.

For some, bringing literacy strategies and skills into other areas of the curriculum seems like an unnecessary add-on. However, these literacy skills and strategies will help students understand both the vocabulary and the concepts in all areas of the curriculum. This practice also enhances their literacy skills and helps students become more aware of the ways in which they learn—certainly not an unnecessary add-on.

9

Supporting Literacy Success for All

"Education is the most powerful weapon which you can use to change the world." — Nelson Mandela

An Antidote to Poverty

Why did *you* become a teacher? I am driven by work that empowers students and teachers, work that I find meaningful. I wholeheartedly believe that words change worlds. Without access to the printed word, it is difficult to fully function in society. And unfortunately, those without literacy skills are more vulnerable to poverty and malnutrition, more likely to be unemployed or underemployed. And because the cycle of poverty persists, many children who live in impoverished homes will come into our classrooms with limited language skills, beginning their formal education at a disadvantage. That's where we come in. Doug Fisher, Nancy Frey, and John Hattie have said, "Literacy is among the major antidotes for poverty." Striving to break the cycle by providing all students will literacy skills is a noble goal indeed. Reading and writing are essential skills. Moats (2020) explains,

> Without well-developed reading skills, children cannot participate fully in classroom learning. They are at much greater risk for school failure and lifelong problems with employment, social adjustment, and personal autonomy. Literate cultures expect literacy of everyone. (7)

As Moats stresses, without adequate literacy skills within our classrooms, students will struggle throughout their schooling and are at greater risk of dropping out of school. Without adequate skills, many will continue to struggle beyond our classrooms. The statistics surrounding literacy rates continue to astound me. According to *ABC Life Literacy Canada*,

> 48% of adult Canadians have literacy skills that fall below a high school level, which negatively affects their ability to function at work and in their personal lives. 17% of Canadians score at or below the lowest level, where they may, for example, be unable

to read the dosage instructions on a medicine bottle. (OECD Programme for the International Assessment of Adult Competencies, 2013)

So when I say I am driven to empower students with literacy skills, I mean *all* students. Not 52%. Not most. All. We know that some students will find the acquisition of literacy skills more challenging than others. This chapter is about supporting those students.

Avoiding the Blame Game

Although you may not remember your own journey in learning to read, you may be privileged to watch your students or your own children on this passage into the literate world. In some ways it is incredible that any of us learn to read when we consider the complexity of this skill. And yet, here you are reading my words. Consider your students… especially those with limited access to the printed word. Are they at fault for their lack of proficiency in this area? Do you blame them or their parents? You may scoff at the questions but I ask them earnestly. We might not consciously blame our students or their parents but we do have to be careful about our unconscious thoughts and certainly the language we use about, and to, students. Robin Bright entitled her book *Sometimes Reading is Hard* for a reason. And she makes an important distinction:

> Notice the difference between these two statements: "Sometimes reading is hard" and "Maria is a struggling reader." When we say the first statement, we help teachers and students understand that challenges are a normal part of reading and that these challenges do not mean there is something wrong with the reader. When we acknowledge that sometimes reading is hard, the implication is that teachers and students can work together to figure out what to do next. (2021, 14)

"The expectations people hold of us often become self-fulfilling prophecies. When others believe in our potential, they give us a ladder. They elevate our aspirations and enable us to reach higher peaks…. In schools, when teachers set high expectations, students get smarter and earn higher grades—especially if they start out with disadvantages." (Grant 2023, 142)

It is essential that we take the mindset Bright suggests when thinking about those who find reading challenging: let's figure out what to do next. Do our expectations about our students' abilities to learn matter? Most certainly. Fisher, Frey, and Hattie (2016) share the results of Hattie's research: "Teachers' expectations of students become the reality for students" (16). A scary thought, but perhaps one that makes sense. If you as a teacher believe that every child can reach their potential, you will do everything you can to help your students succeed. You will continue to embrace your own learning journey and adjust your practice as needed. Unfortunately, Hattie's research shows that the opposite is also true: "Yes, teachers with low expectations are particularly successful at getting what they expect" (16). This is precisely the reason I asked the questions about placing blame. At some point in our career we are likely to have students with poor attendance or a lack of home support. If we blame our students or their parents and presume that these students won't learn, they won't. And sadly, the problems aren't likely to go away. We certainly can't wish them away. But we don't give up on the students because of their circumstances—circumstances usually beyond their control. Instead, we do everything we can to counter the disadvantages they face. Many individuals have overcome the odds against them. Anderson Cooper, Robin Williams, Whoopi Goldberg, and Albert Einstein are among those that struggled with reading and writing as children. And yet, their accomplishments are notable. Anderson Cooper credits his teachers for recognizing his potential and not giving up on him despite his challenges with reading.

Prevention First

The intent of this book is to support teachers in strengthening their universal instruction: instruction aimed at all students. With strong overall instruction, we can provide opportunities that will assist all students on their learning journey and prevent as many students as possible from struggling with literacy skills. There are two optimistic voices I turn to most frequently when thinking about prevention: Kilpatrick and Moats. Kilpatrick (2016) indicates:

> The exciting news is that we can prevent most reading difficulties. Strangely, that is old news among researchers. This prevention phenomenon has been demonstrated in numerous studies over the years, reports of which almost never cross the divide between reading researchers to our K–12 classrooms. (116)

We can prevent most reading difficulties.... That *is* exciting news! So why hasn't the research found its way into the classroom on a wider scale? Sometimes, as teachers, we get into a comfort zone: doing what we do because it's what we've always done or what we were first taught. It takes courage to acknowledge that maybe some of what we've been doing hasn't necessarily been best practice. I've shared some of my regrets with you in hopes that you avoid some of my mistakes. Why did I make those mistakes as a young teacher? I didn't know better at the time. I was doing the best I could with the information I had. But now, with a better understanding of the research, I know I am a better teacher. The more knowledgeable we are about teaching literacy skills, the more effectual we are. Moats (2020) concurs:

> Teachers who are most effective with struggling readers have both content knowledge and practical skill and are more inclined to use direct, systematic, explicit, structured language methods for those who do not learn easily. (xxii)

By learning to provide effective instruction to all students, we will indeed be supporting those most vulnerable. How? Moats (2020) continues:

> According to the convergent findings of numerous studies, classroom instruction that builds phoneme awareness, phonic decoding skills, text reading fluency, vocabulary, and various aspects of comprehension is the best antidote for reading difficulty. (19–20)

Notice the skills she mentions are those discussed in this book at length. Prevention should be our first priority by providing quality, research-proven instruction for all. It may be overwhelming to consider all of the practices you want to implement or the tweaks you want to make to your instruction. Be patient with yourself and do what you can, as you can. Your students will benefit from your thoughtful and intentional practice. Ultimately, when we know better, we do better.

The VAKT Strategy

To help with prevention, another consideration is the VAKT Strategy. This strategy suggests presenting information using multiple senses within your lessons: visual, auditory, and kinesthetic or tactile. In her book *Finding a Place for Every Student*, Cheryll Duquette (2022) explains,

> … most students learn best when the material is presented visually (words, pictures, videos, diagrams, demonstrations), accompanied by oral instruction (auditory), and followed by kinesthetic/tactile (touching, manipulating, printing/writing/typing, doing the task). (26)

I try to incorporate the different modalities into my lessons whenever possible. In fact, you'll notice them in the sample lessons, and in the suggestions to ensure the six strands of language intertwine. Some of the ways we can be intentional about including various modalities are quite simple: writing key words on the board as we say them so students can both see and hear the words, or having students articulate or represent their thinking in a variety of ways. Bringing the tactile component into our classrooms may take a bit more effort. However, as an elementary teacher, I'm sure you recognize the importance of this kinesthetic work for your students. The use of letter tiles, Elkonin boxes, individual whiteboards, materials at literacy stations, and math manipulatives are all ways to ensure students can be physically involved in the tasks. The time spent prepping these materials is time well spent.

When Intervention Is Necessary

Our goal is to reduce the number of students requiring intervention. As we improve our practice with a focus on prevention—implementing changes based on research-proven strategies—we will meet the needs of more and more students. However, there may still be times when intervention is necessary for particular students. The Response to Intervention (RTI) model is often used to guide intervention methods throughout North America. This model includes three tiers.

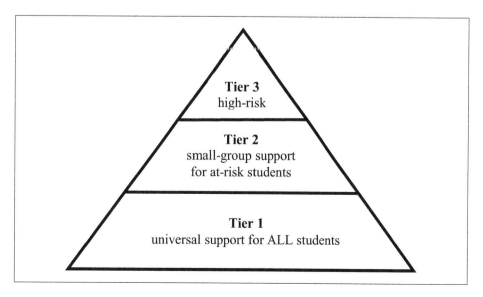

Tier 1 instruction is what we have been addressing throughout this book: the explicit, systematic instruction designed for all students within our classrooms. (Note that Tier 1 instruction should include differentiation for the varying needs of our students.)

Tier 2 refers to small-group intervention. This intervention becomes necessary when students do not make the gains we expect with Tier 1 instruction. Often, this intervention is structured by providing targeted small-group support three to five times each week.

Tier 3 refers to individualized support for our high-risk students.

In his book *Equipped for Reading Success*, Kilpatrick (2016) outlines the types of support provided at each level. He advises, "You will note much overlap between the levels. All involve the key components of orthographic mapping. By its very nature, RTI is just a process and a framework" (123). I highly recommend *Equipped for Reading Success* for intervention teachers. In fact, even if you are not the teacher providing intervention for your students, I recommend reading Kilpatrick's resource. This ensures that instruction is consistent between the tiers and that you as a classroom teacher can reinforce the work of the intervention teacher by using the same strategies in the classroom.

Scheduling Tier 2 and 3 Intervention

If you have students who require Tier 2 or Tier 3 support, it is essential to consider when they receive this intervention. In my experience, intervention often occurs during language arts instruction—the instruction struggling readers need most. In *Reading in the Wild*, Donalyn Miller (2014) expresses her concern:

> When providing reading time at school, we must ensure that all students receive equal access. Administrators, literacy coaches, specialists, and teachers must consider the importance of this reading culture when determining how and when to serve special education and at-risk students. Too often reading intervention specialists pull students who require additional reading support out of class during independent reading time. Disregarding the effect of independent reading time on students' reading achievement undermines our intervention efforts over the long haul. (10)

It's true: those who require more support are often those who do not identify themselves as readers. What's more, they are likely not reading at home. If we take away their independent reading time in the classroom, we are not only taking away an opportunity to practice, we may also be taking away the most valuable opportunity for these students to find a positive association with books. In Chapter 3, we spoke of the importance of choice in reading material during independent reading time. If these students—the very ones who struggle with reading—do not have an opportunity to choose and read books that interest them, we're stepping backward instead of forward.

Through my experience as an intervention teacher, an administrator, and a language arts consultant, I certainly understand the limited resources and time available for intervention. However, without question, intervention should positively impact the students involved. Taking them away from in-class language arts instruction is not ideal. I would also argue that taking them out of subjects they enjoy such as physical education, music, and art is also not ideal. These may be the only moments of the day that these students experience success or joy. Bright (2021) provides an important reminder about our student readers:

"Students who struggle with comprehension are not lazy or unmotivated. They are likely working ridiculously hard but with little success" (128). Intervention may be what's needed to support some students: it is essential, however, that we recognize the emotion entangled in their struggles when scheduling Tier 2 or 3 support.

Intervention support is typically most effective with our youngest students. Whenever possible, we want to identify the gaps early and work to rectify these concerns before the difficulties get more complex. Blevins (2023) also reminds us that effective interventions should "involve well-trained, highly skilled teachers and specialists" and should be "short-lived, lasting only as long as needed" (368). The hope is that as Tier 1 instruction becomes more intentional and explicit, the need for intervention with older students lessens.

Identifying the Gaps

How do we decide the focus of intervention? By getting to know our students as readers. Those *slide in beside* moments that we discussed in Chapter 6 can be revealing and may suggest a need for more support. Screening tools (page 104) can then point us in the right direction as to the type of support. In *Equipped for Reading Success*, Kilpatrick outlines seven skills that can help us understand our students' strengths and weaknesses: oral vocabulary, letter–sound knowledge, phoneme awareness, oral blending, rapid automatized names, working memory, and phonemic decoding. By creating a student profile around these skills, we can address the specific needs of our struggling readers: in essence, this knowledge enables us to teach *the reader*. If we continue to teach *reading* more generally, we might not be targeting the specific needs of the reader, likely reducing the effectiveness of our instruction.

The research shows reason for optimism as we move forward with a better understanding of how to support student readers. Wolf (2007) suggests:

Connecting what we know about the typical child's development to what we know about impediments in reading can help us reclaim the lost potential of millions of children, many of whom have strengths that could light up our lives. (21)

With research at our fingertips, we are now better equipped than ever to support our students—*all* students—in learning to read.

Unfortunately, I have heard teachers voice that particular students will never be able to read. When it comes to working with students, our perspective and expectations are once again important considerations. Kilpatrick (2016) explains:

Rather than labeling students *reading disabled, learning disabled,* or *dyslexic,* it makes more sense to look at what determines skilled reading and find out which skill area or areas are holding these students back.… Would it not make more sense to evaluate these key skill areas and address any weaknesses directly, rather than considering him or her "disabled?" A term like "disabled" implies that the student is destined to struggle in reading. (120)

This deficit model of thinking will not likely lead to the support a student requires to become successful. Rather, we must remember that reading is not innate. Recognizing the research that points to the need for explicit, systematic support for those learning to read is a much more productive perspective.

In their book *Imagine If... Creating a Future for Us All*, Sir Ken Robinson and his daughter Kate Robinson speak to the significant impact we can have on our students' lives:

"The role of teachers is to facilitate students' learning. If you are a teacher, you know that this is not just a job or a profession: it is a calling, and properly conceived, it is an art form. Great teachers don't just know their discipline, they know their students, and they use their expertise to respond to their students' energy and engagement. They are not only instructors, but mentors and guides who can raise the confidence of their students, help them find a sense of direction, and empower them to believe in themselves." (99)

English Language Learners

Learning a new language can be intimidating for many. Creating a positive environment for learning is essential to support risk-taking and honor our students' attempts at language.

Depending on where you teach, your school district may use the term English Language Learners (ELLs), Multilingual Learners (MLs), or English learners (ELs). Regardless of the terminology, it is important to recognize that most students learning English will need some kind of support, simply by virtue of circumstance. Determining the specific needs of these students will propel them more quickly to proficiency. They may require more support with word recognition with direct instruction towards developing phonological awareness, phonemic awareness, and sight-word recognition. We can expect that they will require support with areas within language comprehension—background knowledge, vocabulary, and language structures. As an example, verb tense is often challenging for students learning English and they may need additional support and practice in this area. Moats also suggests a focus on morphology:

English learners (ELs) are especially likely to benefit from explicit instruction in meaningful word parts so that they can infer the meanings of new words encountered in reading. Lacking the range of vocabulary typical of native English speakers, ELs must be shown piece by piece how words are assembled from morphemes and given many opportunities to hear, see, say, and write those elements singly and in combination. (160)

To support our English Language Learners in taking risks when writing, consider using non-permanent methods such as markers on individual whiteboards. Whether breaking down a word, trying to spell a word, or connecting the word to one's other language, working on a whiteboard offers the freedom to take risks and make mistakes.

Did you notice that all of the skills outlined above are skills you will teach to your whole class? The universal strategies discussed throughout this book will support all students in these areas, including those learning English. In many ways, the difference with ELLs is the increase in time, exposure, and practice that may be required to acquire these skills. Consider the important role of oral language for these students too: it acts as a bridge leading to proficiency with the printed word. By establishing practices such as turn-and-talk, all students will have the opportunity to practice language in a safe environment.

Consider your own perspective or potential biases—conscious or unconscious—when working with ELLs. Keep in mind, these students find themselves in a situation beyond their control. Some students may be excited about their new circumstance and learning English. Others may be experiencing trauma or other significant adjustments in their lives; some may even have been separated from family. This seems an appropriate time to remember your students are *humans first*. Yes, we will support them with academic skills, but by acknowledging their circumstances and building relationships, the learning of those academic skills becomes easier.

Translanguaging

When learning another language, we want to encourage students to use their knowledge from one language to support comprehension in the second language. This is known as translanguaging—the English translation of Cen Williams's Welsh term, *trawsieithu* (Conteh, 2018). It is especially effective to capitalize on knowledge of another language when we are deconstructing words during morphology instruction. We can help students see commonalities since words across languages often share an origin and are connected in meaning. As Blevins (2023) reminds us, "Don't forget to use the language skills they already have during your instruction. This asset-based approach is more effective than a deficit-based perspective" (378). It also ensures we recognize our students' strengths. By honoring and connecting to our students' other languages, we remove the potential perceived hierarchy between languages and capitalize on our students' existing linguistic knowledge. An added benefit: students who know another language may begin to see their situation as an advantage rather than a disadvantage. And, since we know how closely emotion is tied to learning, this approach is often empowering.

One of our many jobs as teachers: recognizing and supporting students who find literacy skills challenging. Remember, you have the knowledge and know-how to make a difference and your efforts will have lasting impact.

10

Encouraging Home Literacy Experiences

"When I say to a parent, 'read to a child,' I don't want it to sound like medicine. I want it to sound like chocolate." — Mem Fox

Educating Parents

For simplicity in this chapter I use the term *parents* rather than using *parents or guardians* repeatedly. I encourage you to be aware of your students' home situations and use appropriate language. If some of your students live with guardians other than parents, be inclusive in your language: *parents or grandparents*, for example.

In elementary school, we have considerable contact with parents. Yes, your job is to educate students but you can also help parents or guardians support their children. You may be thinking, *That's not my job*. What I'm suggesting are simple ways to encourage parents to engage their children at home: literacy connections that will ultimately support what you are doing in the classroom. In my current role, I host parent literacy nights to help parents understand how to support their children with literacy skills. When I began presenting to parents, I didn't spend a lot of time on the information that I believed to be common knowledge. However, through the conversations and questions that arose, I've realized that I can't make assumptions: what may be intuitive to some is not to all. This comment is not meant as a judgment, simply a reality given a range of lived experiences and training.

There's no need for you to present an entire literacy evening as I do. But there are ways that you can provide information to parents in the context of what you're already doing. Many schools host a Meet the Teacher Night or some event to kick off the school year, enabling parents to meet their child's teacher. This is a perfect opportunity to give parents a few simple ways to enhance literacy skills at home: establishing a routine of reading aloud, supporting your home reading program, and creating opportunities to practice oral language. Perhaps you send a monthly newsletter to parents or share smaller snippets of information with your parents through social media or another platform such as ClassDojo, School Messenger, or Remind. Perhaps the school website includes a parent page where tips are frequently added. In addition to the logistical information you share regarding hot lunches or field trips, you may also want to share specific strategies that would be helpful for children at the age you teach or quotes about reading and books.

Early on in the school year, I make the effort to call or send a note or email to each of my students' parents sharing something positive about their child. In fact, I make the first calls or send the first notes to those students and their parents who may be surprised to hear something positive. This simple gesture sets a tone for the year ahead, helping to establish relationships with both students and parents.

The Routine of Reading Aloud

The importance of reading aloud to children (of all ages) cannot be overstated. I have realized—through countless conversations and presentations to parents—that many parents believe that there is no reason to read aloud to their children once they become readers themselves. And yet the benefits of reading aloud are many:

- developing phonological awareness, phonemic awareness, and an awareness of print
- increasing vocabulary
- improving understanding of language: structure, grammar, syntax.
- learning self-correction behaviors
- building background knowledge
- practicing oral language skills through conversations about books
- discovering the commonality of experience and develop a sense of empathy
- creating bonds with the adults reading to them

"Children whose parents read to them frequently become familiar with the sophisticated vocabulary and syntax that appears in written rather than spoken language" (Wexler 2019, 34).

It is worth sharing these many benefits of reading aloud with the parents of your students—in my experience, they are often surprised at the extent of the benefits. I encourage parents to carve out time every day to read aloud to their children. For many families, this works best as a bedtime routine. If you are a parent yourself, you might use your own family as an example. Explain that picture books make fantastic read-alouds, as do novels, perhaps reading one or two chapters at a time. Remind parents that even if their children are readers, many of the books we read *to* them are too difficult for our children to read on their own.

Parents who are not confident reading English are often reluctant to read aloud to their children. I remind these parents that there is no shame in learning another language and this may be an opportunity to learn alongside their children. They can take turns reading and their children can share the strategies they are learning in school. When approached with quiet courage, this experience can be empowering and enlightening for all members of the family. I also encourage these parents to read or tell stories in their first language. Your positive approach may lead parents to see their circumstance in a new light.

Encourage Library Visits

Because books are expensive, encourage parents to take their children to the public library. I fondly remember my trips to the library as a child and the thrill of bringing home a stack of "new" books. I continue to be a frequent library user. Children who visit the library are more likely to become adults who visit the library. The library is a way to explore various genres—picture books (fiction and nonfiction), magazines, cookbooks, early chapter books, novels, mysteries, biographies—you name it! The variety of books will help keep children motivated. Routman (2024) speaks to a higher purpose, too:

Public libraries continue to be an oasis for many—a lifeline for communities, families and students with limited or no access to books, content resources, and the broadband and technology services libraries provide. Equitable access to quality, diverse libraries stocked with literature of all types is one of our best hopes for sustaining our fragile democracy. (66)

Some of the parents of your students may not have yet accessed this incredible resource in your community. Do what you can to entice them. For example, on whatever platform you use to communicate with parents, share a "Did you know..." fact about your local public library. Include information about an upcoming event or an available resource, such as Makerspace. Or invite your local public librarian to present at your school—to your classes or to parents. Go one step further: ask the librarian to set up a table to assist families in signing up for library cards on Meet the Teacher Night, Parent-Teacher Interview Night, or during a Demonstration of Learning. Because of the convenience, you will likely have many families sign up. Children are typically excited to get their very own library card.

Home Reading

Above all, emphasize that we want reading at home to be joyful and not a chore. Consider what you can do to ensure your home reading program remains a positive experience for families and does not lead to frustration for either the students or their parents.

On those same evenings I explain to parents the importance of reading aloud to their children, I also explain the purpose of home reading, highlighting the differences between the two. During read-alouds, parents are reading a wide range of text in different genres and at different levels. Home reading, on the other hand, is designed as a way for their *children* to practice reading. Many families do not have access to books at a child's reading level so books from our classrooms can be sent home for this purpose. Will some books disappear from your classroom forever or become damaged on the trips to and from home? Perhaps, but to me it is worth the risk. When students see our own *book love* and how we care for books, they tend to follow our lead.

Do you have a home reading program established for your students? If so, outline your program to parents so they are clear about the reasons and the expectations for home reading. If you teach younger students, your program may be somewhat more formalized: students choose a book to take home each day, read it at home (if possible to a parent or guardian), and return it the next day. If you teach older students, your expectation may be twenty minutes of reading each night from a book of the student's choosing. I have seen teachers insist on a parent signature each day to indicate that their child read at home. I am wary about this expectation as I've seen it lead to considerable anxiety in students. If a parent is worried about putting food on the table for their children, a daily signature may only cause more stress and tension—for both the child and parent. Spend your efforts fostering a love of reading rather than checking signatures.

When you introduce your home reading program to parents, be sure to talk about your goals for your students. If you teach primary students, one of the goals of home reading is likely improved word recognition and fluency. Take this opportunity to talk about the importance of rereading the same book. Parents might not recognize how this practice supports their children with these skills, building confidence along the way. Emphasize that home reading experiences are meant to be positive. If they, as a parent, are concerned about their child's reading, ask them to talk to you rather than voice the concern in front of their child.

One of the ways to generate buy-in for a home reading program is to share statistics with parents about time spent reading. Perhaps you choose to share those on page 36. If our words don't convince parents to support home reading, the statistics often do. Even so, it is important to realize that circumstances vary in each home.

Reading Emergencies

When I listen to students talk, I realize how scheduled their lives have become: evenings and weekends spent at sporting events or music lessons, at their sibling's activities, or in the car on the way to or from said activities. Students might say, "I don't have time to read." And you know, some may be using this as a convenient excuse but others may believe it to be true. And yet, somehow, they spend hours on a phone or other device.

How do we encourage students to find the time to read? I talk to students and parents about Donalyn Miller's idea of "reading emergencies." She asks her students to think about all of the time they spend waiting: "Orthodontist's office, Little sister's soccer game, Sofa shopping with Mom," etc. (Miller 2014, 14–15). What if we had a book to read in these situations? I started bringing a book with me wherever I go, and have been surprised at the many opportunities I find to read. It may not be 20 or 30 minutes of continuous reading, but the 10 minutes here and 15 minutes there certainly add up. Best of all, I no longer mind waiting for my appointments to begin. When I've challenged my students to start taking a book with them—wherever they go—they too express similar results, often saying how fast the time went. When I share this idea with parents, I encourage them to carry a book for themselves and be an example. Rather than defaulting to a device, everyone begins to read more often. This habit may also encourage more frequent library visits.

Oral Language

Students who enter our classrooms with strong oral language skills are at an advantage when it comes to reading and writing. In an extensive, years-long project, Betty Hart and Todd R. Risley studied the talk occurring in the homes of preschoolers. In their book *Meaningful Differences in the Everyday Experience of Young American Children*, they shared this finding:

> Some parents said more than 2,000 words to their child in an average hour together, and others said fewer than 500 words. The data showed that, for each family, the amount the parents talked to their children was so consistent over time that the differences in the children's language experience, mounting up month by month, were enormous by age 3. (xx)

As the title of their book suggests, these are *meaningful differences*. They continue:

"With few exceptions, the more parents talked to their children, the faster the children's vocabularies were growing and the higher the children's IQ test scores at age 3 and later" (xx). With everything we've learned about learning to read, we understand the correlation between the importance of talk in the home and eventual reading comprehension.

From the time they are babies, most children are listening to language. The more opportunities they have to hear diverse talk, the better their foundational skills. This is how they begin to understand the structure of language and all it entails. No one tells a toddler about nouns and verbs, and yet eventually that toddler will begin speaking using various parts of speech. At first the talk will be one or two words at a time. Eventually, most children—if they have considerable exposure to language—intuitively pick up on the structure and conventions of language, mimicking what they hear. Young children will also learn new vocabulary and new information (building background knowledge) from the talk they hear around them. In time, these skills and this knowledge affects their ability to their read.

With parents, I emphasize the importance of talk. Some parents have not considered the importance of oral language in their homes. Ideally, the talk young children hear should be more than functional. The more words and ideas and functions of language children are exposed to, the better! This is true for preschoolers, but we also want parents of school-aged children to keep talking to their children. In part, to continue language development, but regular talk in the home will also contribute to healthy, open relationships. It is important that children feel comfortable talking with their parents, especially as they get older.

During your Meet the Teacher Night or its equivalent, explain to parents that you are going to give their child oral language homework—often. If you first share the importance of oral language, parents are more apt to understand the benefits and realize your intention through this assignment. Explain that you want their child to be able to articulate their thinking and learning, and to answer questions about the topic. Because I am transparent with my students, they know that this is a way to enhance their learning: we've talked about the importance of talk! The child's homework assignment will begin with *"Tell your parents about…"* and then include something specific such as *the book we read today*; *the science experiment about condensation*; or *the new morpheme you learned, its meaning, and words using that morpheme.* Anything! I give this assignment to children as young as Kindergarten. If we've read a book and completed a reader response, I will explain to students that their homework is to *"Tell your parents about the book we read and your favorite part!"* With older students learning about structures in science, I might say *"Tell your parents what makes a structure more stable."* As much as possible, I want the child to take initiative but we know that doesn't always happen. So use your existing communication platform to tell parents what to ask if their child doesn't volunteer the information: *"Ask your child about the book we read today and their favorite part!"*

I've had many parents over the years who have told me how this practice transformed the talk in their homes: it became a way to engage with their child's learning in meaningful ways. Many parents extend these conversations and learn how to better engage their children in talk.

Family Game Nights

Another fantastic way to encourage talk in the home is through family game nights. A considerable amount of learning occurs during our interactions while playing games: turn-taking, reading, counting, vocabulary development, and of course the inevitable conversation. The games themselves matter less than the opportunities to play. I often suggest card games because of the limited expense of a deck of cards. As for board games, consider suggesting some that would be age-appropriate to the grade level you are teaching: Blank Slate, Guess Who?, Hedbanz, Kerplunk, Sequence for Kids, Sequence, Taboo Junior, and Telestrations.

Give this oral language homework to your students multiple times each week.
Tell your parents about…
Explain to your parents…
Notice the topics can be from any area of the curriculum!

Dinner Table Talk

Families are busy. Even still, I encourage parents to make mealtime, talk time whenever possible. Parents often share their frustration when they ask their child about the school day: *"How was your day?"*—*"Good.";* *"What did you learn today?"*—*"Nothing."* Encourage parents to try these questions instead: *"What was the best part of your day?" "Did you raise your hand in class today?" "What was challenging about today?"*

In addition to talk about the day, we can also engage children with prompts or questions such as "If you…", "What if…", or "Would you rather…"

- "If you could have one superpower, what would you choose?"
- "If you could invent anything, what would you invent?"
- "What if [your pet's name] could talk? How would our lives be different?"
- "What would you do if your best friend was being bullied?"
- "Would you rather learn how to cook or to drive?"
- "Would you rather be stuck in a room with a bumblebee or a racoon?"

It isn't so much the question that matters, it is the opportunity to think creatively and critically, to articulate their thinking, and learn to listen to other family members. As you can predict from the prompts, some will lead to hilarious conversations and others might be quite thoughtful. As children get familiar with these question starters, they will often create their own questions. In fact, if you try these prompts in the classroom, you could encourage your students to initiate the conversation at home.

Quotations to Inspire

Words can inspire, set a tone, and reveal your priorities. Periodically, share a quotation with the parents of your students, reminding them of the importance of books and reading. Share your favorites or consider these:

- "A book is a gift you can open again and again."—Garrison Keillor
- "Today a reader, tomorrow a leader."—Margaret Fuller
- "Reading should not be presented to children as a chore, a duty. It should be offered as a gift."—Kate DiCamillo
- "We read to know we are not alone."—C.S. Lewis
- "Reading is a way for me to expand my mind, open my eyes, and fill up my heart."—Oprah Winfrey
- "Reading is to the mind what exercise is to the body."—Joseph Addison
- "The only thing that you absolutely have to know, is the location of the library."—Albert Einstein
- "What a blessing it is to love books."—Elizabeth von Arnim
- "I read to become more hopeful, to glimpse what might be possible, to be exposed to universal human experiences, to understand other cultures and other lives, to see myself and my life more clearly."—Regie Routman

As You Close This Book...

Each time you enter your classroom, I encourage you to think of it as an opportunity: an opportunity to empower your students with a wealth of literacy skills, skills they will use every day of their lives. When we strive to build meaningful relationships with students, we will ultimately have a more significant impact on their learning. By embracing our own learning journey, being open to making changes in our practice, and acknowledging our hidden biases, we put our best selves in front of our students.

Make the most of your opportunity with students: literacy instruction matters.

Glossary

Active View of Reading: a model of reading introduced in 2021 by Nell Duke and Kelly Cartwright. This model shows the interaction between the two elements of the Simple View of Reading (word recognition and language comprehension), and also demonstrates how active self-regulation and executive functioning play a role in effective reading. See page 58.

Alphabetic Principle: the understanding that there are predictable relationships between written letters and spoken sounds. See page 70.

Anchor Chart: a tool used to support instruction and "anchor" the learning for students. Anchor charts are often co-constructed with students. See page 18.

Articulatory Gestures: noticing what our mouth, lips, and tongue are doing as we produce a specific sound or phoneme. See page 17.

Base Element: a morpheme that is the structural foundation of a word and provides the core meaning; base element is an umbrella term that includes both *bases* (words in and of themselves such as *use* or *friend*) and *roots* (which require another morpheme to become a word such as *ject* or *struct*). See page 79.

Blend: two letters that come together but each letter maintains their individual sounds; e.g., *fr, st, gl, sw*. See page 74.

Blending: combining phonemes to create a word; e.g., /d/ /i/ /g/ = dig. See page 73.

Concepts of Print: the understanding that text holds meaning, that letters form words, that print is read from top to bottom and left to right, how pages are turned, and so on. See page 89.

Decoding: the ability to apply knowledge of letter–sound relationships to correctly pronounce written words. See page 57.

Digraph: two letters that come together to create a new sound; e.g., *sh, wh, th, ph*. See page 74.

Elkonin Boxes: an instructional tool used to help children improve their phonemic awareness by segmenting words into individual phonemes. See page 75.

Encoding: the ability to apply knowledge of letter–sound relationships to write words. See page 63.

Etymology: the study of the origin and history of words. See page 79.

Grapheme: the written representation of one sound (a letter or combination of letters). See page 74.

High-Frequency Words: the words most commonly used in the English language. They can be phonetically regular (e.g., *in, it, and, can, went*) or irregular (e.g., *the, of, have, was, should*). See page 15.

Morpheme: the smallest unit of meaning within a word. *Free morphemes* can stand alone; e.g., *girl, big, sleep. Bound morphemes* cannot stand alone or be used as an independent word. There are three types of bound morphemes that we teach our students: prefixes, suffixes, and roots. See page 77.

Morphology: the study of words, how they are formed, and how they relate to other words. See page 77.

Onset: the initial sound of any word; e.g., /d/ in *dog*, /tw/ in *twin*. See page 72.

Orthographic Mapping: the process used in the brain to map words (spelling, pronunciation, and meaning) into memory. See page 81.

Phoneme: the smallest unit of sound within a word. See page 72.

Phonemic Awareness: the awareness that words are made up of distinct sounds (phonemes). It is one subset of *phonological awareness*. See page 72.

Phonics: the knowledge that sounds (*phonemes*) are represented by letters or letter combinations (*graphemes*). See page 74.

Phonological Awareness: an awareness of the sound structure of words. It is an umbrella term that includes such subsets as *phonemic awareness, syllables, onset,* and *rime*. See page 72.

Plot Patterns: patterns in the stories we read and write; e.g., transformation stories, circle stories, stuck stories, quest stories, competition stories. See page 117.

Prosody: the ability to read with expression, including elements such as phrasing, pitch, rhythm, intonation, tone, and emphasis. See page 94.

Rime: the string of letters that follow the onset sound; e.g., /og/ in *dog*, /in/ in *twin*. See page 72.

Scarborough's Reading Rope: Dr. Hollis Scarborough published this graphic in 2001, detailing the specific strands required to become a skilled reader; see visual on page 58.

Science of Reading: an extensive body of research on how our brains learn to read that includes scientific knowledge from experts in disciplines such as education, literacy, educational psychology, developmental psychology, and neurology. See page 71.

Segmentation: breaking a word apart into phonemes; e.g., *dad* = /d/ /a/ /d/. See page 80.

Sight Words: words that are instantly recalled from memory; they can be phonically regular or irregular. See page 80.

Sight-Word Vocabulary: each person's own set of vocabulary that they recognize from memory.

Simple View of Reading: a theory proposed in 1986 by Philip Gough and William Tunmer: *Word Recognition x Language Comprehension = Reading Comprehension*. See page 57.

Trigraph: three letters that come together to create a single sound; e.g., *air, igh, tch, dge*. See page 74.

Recommended Resources

For Teaching Reading

Beers, Kylene, and Robert E. Probst. 2017. *Disrupting Thinking: Why How We Read Matters.* New York, NY: Scholastic.

Bright, Robin. 2021. *Sometimes Reading is Hard: Using decoding, vocabulary, and comprehension strategies to inspire fluent, passionate, lifelong readers.* Markham, ON: Pembroke Publishers.

Burkins, Jan, and Kari Yates. 2021. *Shifting the Balance: 6 Ways to Bring the Science of Reading into the Balanced Literacy Classroom.* Portsmouth, NH: Stenhouse Publishers.

Cunningham, Katie Egan, Jan Burkins, and Kari Yates. 2024. *Shifting the Balance: 6 Ways to Bring the Science of Reading into the Upper Elementary Classroom.* Portsmouth, NH: Stenhouse Publishers.

Daniels, Harvey. 2002. *Literature Circles: Voice and Choice in Book Clubs & Reading Groups.* Portland, ME: Stenhouse Publishers.

Miller, Donalyn. 2009. *The Book Whisperer: Awakening the Inner Reader in Every Child.* San Francisco, CA: Jossey-Bass.

Miller, Donalyn. 2014. *Reading in the Wild: The Book Whisperer's Keys to Cultivating Lifelong Reading Habits.* San Francisco, CA: Jossey-Bass.

For Teaching Writing

Culham, Ruth. 2003. *6+1 Traits of Writing: The Complete Guide Grades 3 and Up.* New York, NY: Scholastic.

Culham, Ruth. 2005. *6+1 Traits of Writing: The Complete Guide for the Primary Grades.* New York, NY: Scholastic.

Filewych, Karen. 2017. *How Do I Get Them to Write? Explore the reading–writing connection using freewriting and mentor texts to motivate and empower students.* Markham, ON: Pembroke Publishers.

Filewych, Karen. 2017. *Freewriting with Purpose: Simple classroom techniques to help students make connections, think critically, and construct meaning.* Markham, ON: Pembroke Publishers.

For Teaching Phonemic Awareness and Phonics

Blevins, Wiley. 2023. *Teaching Phonics & Word Study in the Intermediate Grades.* Third Edition. New York, NY: Scholastic.

Georgiou, George, and Kristy Dunn. 2023. *The Phonics Companion: 120 Lessons for Teachers.* Toronto, ON: Pearson Canada.

"The Heggerty Phonemic Awareness Curriculum." *Heggerty*, heggerty.org/programs/phonemic-awareness/.

Willms, Heather, and Giacinta Alberti. 2022. *This Is How We Teach Reading… And It's Working!: The What, Why, and How of Teaching Phonics in K-3 Classrooms.* Markham, ON: Pembroke Publishers.

For Teaching Word Study and Vocabulary

Allen, Janet. 2007. *Inside Words: Tools for teaching academic vocabulary, grades 4–12.* Portsmouth, NH: Stenhouse Publishers.

Beck, Isabel, Margaret McKeown, and Linda Kucan. 2013. *Bringing Words to Life: Robust Vocabulary Instruction.* New York, NY: The Guilford Press.

Filewych, Karen. 2024. *Bug Club Morphology: Kits A, B, C, D.* Toronto, ON: Pearson Canada.

Marzano, Robert J., and Debra J. Pickering. 2005. *Building Academic Vocabulary: Teacher's Manual.* Association for Supervision & Curriculum Development.

Swartz, Larry. 2019. *Word by Word: 101 ways to inspire and engage students by building vocabulary, improving spelling, and enriching reading, writing, and learning.* Markham, ON: Pembroke Publishers.

For General Instruction and Best Practice

Almarode, John, and Kara Vandas. 2019. *Clarity for Learning: Five Essential Practices that Empower Students and Teachers.* Thousand Oaks, CA: Corwin.

Fisher, Douglas, Nancy Frey, and John Hattie. 2017. *Teaching Literacy in the Visible Learning Classroom.* Thousand Oaks, CA: Corwin.

"PZ's Thinking Routines Toolbox." *Project Zero*, pz.harvard.edu/thinking-routines.

Ritchhart, Ron, Mark Church, and Karin Morrison. 2011. *Making Thinking Visible: How to Promote Engagement, Understanding, and Independence for All Learners.* San Francisco, CA: Jossey-Bass.

Routman, Regie. 2024. *The Heart-Centered Teacher: Restoring Hope, Joy, and Possibility in Uncertain Times.* New York, NY: Routledge.

For Literacy Intervention

Kilpatrick, David. 2016. *Equipped for Reading Success: A Comprehensive, Step-by-Step Program for Developing Phonemic Awareness and Fluent Word Recognition.* Syracuse, NY: Casey & Kirsch Publishers.

Moats, Louisa, C. 2020. *Speech to Print: Language Essentials for Teachers.* Third Edition. Baltimore, MD: Paul H. Brookes Publishing Co.

References

ABC Life Literacy Canada. 2024. www.abclifeliteracy.ca/literacy-at-a-glance/

Adams, Marilyn J. 1994. *Beginning to Read: Thinking and Learning about Print.* Cambridge, MA: MIT Press.

Alberta Education. 2022. *English Language Arts and Literature.* Edmonton, AB: Alberta Education.

Allington, Richard, and Rachael Gabriel. 2012. "Every Child, Every Day." *ACSD, 69 (6).* www.ascd.org/el/articles/every-child-every-day

Almarode, John, and Kara Vandas. 2019. *Clarity for Learning: Five Essential Practices that Empower Students and Teachers.* Thousand Oaks, CA: Corwin.

"A Note About Reading Levels." *Fountas & Pinnell Literacy,* HMH Education Company, fpblog. fountasandpinnell.com/a-note-about-reading-levels#:~:text=When%20children%20select%20 books%20from,'t%20have%20to)%20understand.

Beck, Isabel, Margaret McKeown, and Linda Kucan. 2013. *Bringing Words to Life: Robust Vocabulary Instruction.* New York, NY: The Guilford Press.

Beers, Kylene, and Robert E. Probst. 2017. *Disrupting Thinking: Why How We Read Matters.* New York, NY: Scholastic.

Bishop, Rudine Sims. 1990. "Mirrors, Windows, and Sliding Glass Doors." *Perspectives: Choosing and Using Books for the Classroom,* vol. 6, no. 3. Summer 1990.

Blevins, Wiley. 2023. *Teaching Phonics & Word Study in the Intermediate Grades.* Third Edition. New York, NY: Scholastic.

Borba, Michele. 2016. *Unselfie: Why Empathetic Kids Succeed in Our All-About-Me World.* New York, NY: Touchstone.

Bright, Robin. 2021. *Sometimes Reading is Hard: Using decoding, vocabulary, and comprehension strategies to inspire fluent, passionate, lifelong readers.* Markham, ON: Pembroke Publishers.

Burkins, Jan, and Kari Yates. 2021. *Shifting the Balance: 6 Ways to Bring the Science of Reading into the Balanced Literacy Classroom.* Portsmouth, NH: Stenhouse Publishers.

Conteh, Jean. 2018. "Translanguaging." *ELT Journal,* 72(4), 445–447. www.academic.oup.com/eltj/article/72/4/445/5098484

Cunningham, Anne, and Keith Stanovich. 1998. "What Reading Does for the Mind." *American Educator,* Spring/Summer.

Daniels, Harvey, and Steven Zemelman. 2014. *Subjects Matter: Exceeding Standards Through Powerful Content-Area Reading.* Portsmouth, NH: Heinemann.

Dehaene, Stanislas. 2010. *Reading in the Brain: The New Science of How We Read.* New York, NY: Penguin Group.

Duke and Cartwright. "The Active View of Reading." Nell K. Duke, Nell K. Duke, Early Literacy Research, Policy, & Practice, www.nellkduke.org/the-active-view-of-reading

Duquette, Cheryll. 2022. *Finding a Place for Every Student: Inclusion practices, social belonging, and differentiated instruction in elementary classrooms.* Markham, ON: Pembroke Publishers.

Eide, Denise. 2012. *Uncovering the Logic of English: A Common-Sense Approach to Reading, Spelling, and Literacy.* Rochester, MN: Logic of English, Inc.

Elbow, Peter. 1998. *Writing With Power: Techniques for Mastering the Writing Process.* New York, NY: Oxford University Press, Inc.

Fisher, Douglas, Nancy Frey, and John Hattie. 2016. *Visible Learning for Literacy: Implementing the Practices That Work Best to Accelerate Student Learning.* Thousand Oaks, CA: Corwin.

Fisher, Douglas, Nancy Frey, and John Hattie. 2017. *Teaching Literacy in the Visible Learning Classroom.* Thousand Oaks, CA: Corwin.

Fountas, Irene C., and Gay Su Pinnell. 2016. *The Fountas & Pinnell Literacy Continuum, Expanded Edition: A Tool for Assessment, Planning, and Teaching, Prek-8.* Portsmouth, NH: Heinemann.

Fox, Mem. 1993. *Radical Reflections: Passionate Opinions on Teaching, Learning and Living.* New York: Harcourt Brace.

Government of Newfoundland and Labrador. 2014. *English Language Arts.* Department of Education.

Government of Nova Scotia. 2019. *English Language Arts.* Halifax: Department of Education and Early Childhood Development.

Grant, Adam. 2023. *Hidden Potential: The Science of Achieving Great Things.* New York: Viking.

Hammond, W. Dorsey. 2024. "Reading Legislation: An Alarming Development." Posted at www.literacytalk. info/our-perspectives-on-key-issues.

Hart, Betty, and Todd R. Risley. 2011. *Meaningful Differences in the Everyday Experience of Young American Children.* Baltimore, MD: Paul H. Brookes Publishing Co.

Hart, Melissa. 2019. *Better with Books: 500 Diverse Books to Ignite Empathy and Encourage Self-Acceptance in Tween and Teens.* Seattle, WA: Sasquatch Books.

Heard, Georgia. 2016. *Heart Maps: Helping Students Create and Craft Authentic Writing.* Portsmouth, NH: Heinemann.

Institute for Multi-Sensory Education. 2017. "12 Famous People Who Struggled with Dyslexia Before Changing the World." journal.imse.com/12-famous-people-who-struggled-with-dyslexia-before-changing-the-world/

Johns, Jerry L., and Kristine H. Wilke. 2018. "High-Frequency Words: Some Ways to Teach and Help Students Practice and Learn Them." *Texas Journal of Literacy Education,* 6 (1).

Johnson, Brad, and Hal Bowman. 2021. *Dear Teacher: 100 Days of Inspirational Quotes and Anecdotes.* New York, NY: Routledge.

Kilpatrick, David. 2016. *Equipped for Reading Success: A Comprehensive, Step-by-Step Program for Developing Phonemic Awareness and Fluent Word Recognition.* Syracuse, NY: Casey & Kirsch Publishers.

Miller, Donalyn. 2009. *The Book Whisperer: Awakening the Inner Reader in Every Child.* San Francisco, CA: Jossey-Bass.

Miller, Donalyn. 2014. *Reading in the Wild: The Book Whisperer's Keys to Cultivating Lifelong Reading Habits.* San Francisco, CA: Jossey-Bass.

Moats, Louisa, C. 2020. *Speech to Print: Language Essentials for Teachers.* Third Edition. Baltimore, MD: Paul H. Brookes Publishing Co.

Newkirk, Thomas. 2023. *Literacy's Democratic Roots: A personal Tour Through 8 Big Ideas.* Portsmouth, NH: Heinemann.

Ontario Curriculum and Resources. 2023. *Elementary Language.* www.dcp.edu.gov.on.ca/en/curriculum/elementary-language.

Ouellette, Gene P. 2006. "What's Meaning Got to Do With It: The Role of Vocabulary in Word Reading and Reading Comprehension." *Journal of Educational Psychology,* 98 (3): 554-566.

Pearson, P. David, and Margaret C. Gallagher. 1983. "The Instruction of Reading Comprehension." *Contemporary Educational Psychology,* 8 (3): 317–44.

Ritchhart, Ron, Mark Church, and Karin Morrison. 2011. *Making Thinking Visible: How to Promote Engagement, Understanding, and Independence for All Learners.* San Francisco, CA: Jossey-Bass.

Roberts, Kate. 2018. *A Novel Approach: Whole-Class Novels, Student-Centered Teaching, and Choice.* Portsmouth, NH: Heinemann.

Robinson, Sir Ken, and Kate Robinson. 2022. *Imagine If…: Creating a Future for Us All.* New York, NY: Penguin Books.

Routman, Regie. 2024. *The Heart-Centered Teacher: Restoring Hope, Joy, and Possibility in Uncertain Times.* New York, NY: Routledge.

Routman, Regie. 2014. *Read, Write, Lead: Breakthrough Strategies for Schoolwide Literacy Success.* Alexandria, VA: ASCD.

Seidenberg, Mark. 2018. *Language at the Speed of Sight: How We Read, Why So Many Can't, and What Can Be Done About It.* New York, NY: Basic Books.

Wexler, Natalie. 2019. *The Knowledge Gap: The Hidden Cause of America's Broken Education System—And How to Fix It.* New York, NY: Avery.

Willingham, Daniel T. 2017. *The Reading Mind: A Cognitive Approach to Understanding How the Mind Reads.* San Francisco, CA: Jossey-Bass.

Wolf, Maryanne. 2007. *Proust and the Squid: The Story and Science of the Reading Brain.* New York, NY: HarperCollins Publishers.

Index